HOLY POWER,
HUMAN PAIN

TO JEAN
*whose constant encouragement, sound advice,
and generous assistance
brought this project to fruition.*

HOLY POWER, HUMAN PAIN

Richard F. Vieth

MEYER STONE BOOKS

Published in the United States by Meyer-Stone Books, a division of Meyer, Stone, and Company, Inc., 2014 South Yost Avenue, Bloomington, IN 47403

Cover design: Terry Dugan Design

Typesetting output: TEXSource, Houston

Manufactured in the United States of America
92 91 90 89 88   5 4 3 2 1

Library of Congress Cataloging in Publication Data

Vieth, Richard F., 1927–
  Holy power, human pain.

  Includes index.
  1. Theodicy.   2. Suffering — Religious aspects —
Christianity.   I. Title.
BT160.V54   1988   231'.8   88-42727
ISBN 0-940989-42-5

Contents

1 "God It Hurts!":
Pain, Suffering, and the Threat to Human Meaning   **1**

Murder in Prospect   *2*
Cassell's Definition of Suffering   *5*
Types of Suffering   *6*
Oppression   *9*
Suffering and Soul-making   *11*
Suffering and the Quest for Meaning   *13*

2 "Why, God?":
Omnipotence Reconsidered   **17**

"God Planned This Accident"   *20*
Theological Responses   *23*
Responses Rejecting or Redefining Omnipotence   *24*
     Response One: Dualism, 26; Response Two: Satan, 28;
     Response Three: Natural Order, 31; Response Four: Free Choice, 33

3 "Where Is God?":
Holiness Reconsidered   **39**

Responses Rejecting or Redefining Divine Benevolence   *39*
     Response Five: Despotism, 39; Response Six: Judgment, 42;
     Response Seven: Testing, 45; Response Eight: Personal Growth, 46

Responses Denying or Redefining Evil   *50*
     Response Nine: Illusion, 50; Response Ten: Partial Perspective, 51

Atheism and Agnosticism   *53*
     Response Eleven: Atheism, 53; Response Twelve: Mystery, 54

A Personal Conclusion   *55*

4 "The Devil Made Me Do It"
Demonic Power and Human Responsibility   **59**

Defining Evil   *59*

Social Evil and Social Research   *64*

My Lai   *68*

Nazi Doctors   *71*

National Socialism as "Applied Biology," 73; Institutionalizing
the Vision, 74; Psychological Patterns Conducive to Evil: Doubling, 76;
The Human Face of Evil, 79

"We Have Met the Enemy..."   *82*

5 "My God, My God...":
Holy Passion and Compassion   **86**

Biblical Roots   *87*

Classical Theism   *89*

Contemporary Revisions   *92*

Alfred North Whitehead, 92; Abraham Heschel, 96;
Jürgen Moltmann, 99

God and the Lone Ranger   *104*

6 We Shall Overcome:
Human Communion in Affliction and Joy   **110**

Presence   *110*

Phases of Affliction   *114*

Phase One: Impact, 115; Phase Two: Working Through, 117;
Phase Three: Changing, 120

Resistance   *123*

Liturgy   *132*

Notes   **138**

Index   **149**

"God It Hurts!":
Pain, Suffering, and
the Threat to Human Meaning

In recent years there has been growing interest in the problem of suffering. People want to understand it in order to deal better with their own afflictions, and also to help others cope more effectively with theirs. People are also groping for ways to put seemingly pointless pain into some larger perspective that will redeem its value.

This heightened attentiveness to suffering can be seen in the annual flood of new publications on the subject, including Rabbi Kushner's best seller, which millions of lay people have found helpful, despite early critical neglect.[1] My own interest in this subject has been triggered by the intense concern of my students — seminarians, clergy, and laity — many of whom have an urgent personal stake in the topic.

This recent interest may seem surprising, when we consider the perennial nature of the problem. Already 2,500 years ago, Aeschylus addressed the issue when he wrote,

> [Zeus] setting us on the road
> Made this a valid law —
>   "That men must learn by suffering."

One can only speculate about the reasons for the current preoccupation with this topic. A first possibility is that our century, in contrast to the optimism in which it was born, has become a maelstrom of violence and travail, from World War I to the Holocaust, to the "killing fields" of Cambodia, to the current epidemics of domestic violence and worldwide torture. A second possible reason is widespread disaffection with traditional answers that counsel patient acceptance of affliction as God's will. "We've turned tradition on its head," says Maryknoll missionary Richard Ouellette. "It used to be God's will to accept the suffering. Now it's God's will to denounce the suffering."[2] A third possible reason is disillusionment with the god of medical technology, which was expected to eradicate suffering, or at least transmute pain into euphoria through chemistry.

If human suffering, far from being eliminated, has actually increased in this century, while hoary answers no longer work, then it is time to re-examine the issues. This volume will do that by investigating the nature of human suffering, relating it to God on the one hand and evil on the other, and by exploring the resources of faith for healing human suffering. In this chapter we will define suffering and describe its types, examine its relationship to pain and evil, and note the reciprocal impact of suffering and religious faith on each other.

Murder in Prospect

We begin with a concrete example. In 1978 the following story from Prospect, Conn., appeared in newspapers all across the country:

> Eight victims of the worst mass murder in the state's history, a young mother and her seven children, were buried side by side Wednesday in a plot shaded by maple trees at a cemetery as old as this small, 150-year-old Connecticut town.
>
> Thirty-four pallbearers carried the caskets to the Prospect Town Cemetery just across the road from the church — six pallbearers for 29-year-old Cheryl Beaudoin and four for each of her children.
>
> "How could something like this happen?" the Rev. Joseph Donnelly asked friends and relatives who crowded the 850-seat St. Anthony Padua Roman Catholic Church to mourn the death of Mrs. Beaudoin and her children.
>
> "Why does God let this go on? Why do the innocent suffer? And yet, as surely as we have all asked these questions, we have all found that there are no answers — none at all."

> Mrs. Beaudoin, her children and 6-year-old Jennifer Santorto, a friend who was spending the night, were slain on Friday, and their house in this quiet community of 7,000 was burned to the ground.
>
> Mrs. Beaudoin's husband, Frederick, 33, was at work at the time. His foster brother, Lorne J. Acquin, 27, has been charged with arson and nine counts of murder in the slayings.
>
> "The events of these past days point out to all of us again the fact that there is evil in this world," Father Donnelly said during the funeral mass at the church where the Beaudoins were married a dozen years ago and where each of their children was baptized.
>
> "It is an evil that man inflicts on himself and his world whenever he fails to respect God, himself or his fellow man. The meaning of what has happened has deeply affected all of us."
>
> At the end of the service, Father Donnelly sprinkled holy water on Mrs. Beaudoin's white, plush-finished casket and the white metal caskets of the children to symbolize the sacrament of baptism through water. The caskets were then blessed with incense to show respect and reverence for the dead.[3]

As an avenue into understanding suffering, let us begin by identifying the feelings that would have been present among those attending that funeral. What would the relatives, friends, and neighbors of the Beaudoins have felt as they participated in the final service for the murdered family? Surely there would have been grief at the tragic loss, grief accentuated by its suddenness and the horrendous manner in which it came about. Certainly also there would have been anger: indignation against the perpetrator of this crime and perhaps also resentment toward his foster brother, Frederick Beaudoin, surviving father in the slain family. Doubtless some would have blamed him for allowing his foster brother to commit the crime. Others might have blamed the police for not preventing it, and surely some would have blamed God. Finding someone to blame, it seems, helps persons get rational control over an otherwise irrational disaster. For his own part, Frederick Beaudoin, the sole survivor out of this family of nine, would have had his own double load of

guilt to handle. "If only . . . ," he must have thought to himself a
thousand times, and "Why not *me?*" — the question that haunts
every survivor.

Others present would have been asking a different "why not"
question. "If this could happen to the Beaudoins, then why not
to *me?*" Suddenly the foundation crumbles beneath our secure
world as we are confronted by our mortality. "Contingency," the
medievals called it: I might be, or I might not be. No necessity
guarantees my continued existence beyond this moment. "Dust
in the wind, all we are is dust in the wind," keens the rock group.
The only way to ward off this anxiety of insecurity is denial: "It
couldn't happen to me."

And what of Father Donnelly? Any pastor will understand
his sense of shock at what has transpired, his spiritual anguish
in trying to find God in this horrendous event, and his feeling of emptyhandedness in the face of his people's need. He
has no magic to bring back the dead, no medicine to ease the
hurt of the living. He is simply a servant of the word, so he
uses that gift to give voice to the congregation's shock and outrage, thereby giving them permission to express what they are
feeling and thinking. "How could something like this happen?"
he protests, speaking for them all. And then, letting the complaint ascend to heaven, he asks, "Why does God let this go
on?" These shocking events, he is acknowledging, call into question the very One who guarantees life's goodness and insures its
purpose. For people who are hurting, the deepest anguish is often the disintegration of the framework of meaning that gives
life its worth, and the ensuing struggle to put something in its
place.

What feelings would have been present on that occasion?
Surely grief, anger, guilt, fear, and spiritual distress. These are
the hurts that characterize human suffering at the scene of any
tragedy like this. They are the forms of mental anguish. But
don't we usually associate suffering with *physical* pain rather
than mental distress, even using "pain" and "suffering" interchangeably? When we hear the word "suffering," isn't the picture that pops into mind something like the excruciating pain
of a cancer patient or the agonizing screams of a torture victim?
Isn't real suffering physical pain, and only in a secondary and
derivative sense the psychological anguish that accompanies and
somehow mimics it?

Cassell's Definition of Suffering

This way of thinking has been sharply challenged by Eric J. Cassell, M.D., in a monograph entitled, "The Nature of Suffering and the Goals of Medicine."[4] Cassell believes that too many physicians misconstrue the nature of suffering and consequently mistreat their patients. It is not *bodies* that suffer, Cassell contends, nor is it *minds*. Rather, "suffering is experienced by *persons*."[5] Human beings are, to be sure, multi-dimensional, and suffering can originate or focus in any of the many facets of personhood, but it is the whole person, the centered self, that suffers. Any treatment of human suffering that does not consider it holistically will therefore be inadequate and perhaps even harmful.

How, then, should suffering be interpreted? "Suffering," Cassell claims, "occurs when an impending destruction of the person is perceived."[6] Suffering is the anguish felt in the face of a severe threat to the very core of our being, a threat to our "intactness" or "integrity." The threat is the possibility of disintegration of the self. Our daily language reflects this when we say, "I'm going to pieces," or "She's breaking apart at the seams," or "He's coming unglued."

The threat may be literally to one's life, through terminal illness or fatal injury, or it may be to one's meaning and worth, through loss of work, or home, or spouse, or "face." To fit Cassell's criterion, the perceived danger must be significant, not trivial, and in this regard his meaning is narrower than our common usage. We say, "I'm suffering from the heat today," even when we don't experience the temperature as life-threatening. Cassell has something more serious in mind. Furthermore, the danger must be perceived as life-threatening *by the one who is suffering*. What is perceived by one person as life-endangering may be viewed by another as a bracing challenge.[7]

This brings us to Cassell's definition. "Most generally," he says, "suffering can be defined as the state of severe distress associated with events that threaten the intactness of the person."[8] "Distress" is an apt term to describe the inner strain corresponding to an external threat of disintegration, for "dis-tress" means literally "to pull apart." Furthermore, Webster reminds us that distress can mean "anguish of *body or mind*,"[9] thus preserving the holism of the concept. Suffering, then, is a state of severe

distress triggered by events perceived to threaten destruction
of a person's intactness or wholeness. That distress, according
to Cassell, will find emotional expression in such specific feelings as sadness, anger, loneliness, depression, grief, unhappiness,
melancholy, rage, withdrawal, and yearning.[10]

Types of Suffering

What are the kinds of events in human life that seriously imperil
our intactness? Cassell lists pain, injury, and loss — the same
ones included in most dictionary definitions. To these I will add
a fourth: oppression.

The first is *pain.* We have carefully drawn a distinction between physical pain and suffering, but certain forms of physical
pain can threaten to destroy a person in the very way Cassell
has in mind. He lists four kinds of pain that have this potential: pain that is *overwhelming,* pain that seems *endless,* pain
whose *source is unknown,* and pain that *signals a dire consequence.* These kinds of pain can tear us apart. "It's only a
headache," people say, but migraine or cluster headaches can
be overwhelming and endless, their cause difficult to pinpoint.
When that happens, the victim can begin to think, "I have a
brain tumor." Thus even a "mere headache" can fit Cassell's
criteria for pain that produces suffering. Extreme pain makes
the victim feel that he or she has lost control and will never
be able to regain it. If the pain can be brought under control,
then the suffering will be reduced, if not resolved. Often, Cassell
adds, even the pain itself will be diminished when the patient
recognizes that it has been brought under control.[11]

An illustration is provided by a seminarian with severe and
continuous back pain that made walking or even travelling by
car extremely uncomfortable. Because the source of pain could
not be located, no procedure could be prescribed that would end
the pain and restore mobility. This in turn cast a dark shadow
across the future ministry to which she believed herself called.
Thus her pain corresponded to all four types mentioned by Cassell as inducing suffering. When finally a bone fusion was recommended as a possible solution, she jumped at the opportunity,
even though the surgical procedure involved significant risk of
paralysis. Surgery held out at least the possibility of an end to
her pain and thus revived the dream of fulfilling her calling.

Even before surgery, her distress was lessened because she had regained partial control over the pain.

A second cause of suffering is *injury.* All of us know persons who have survived an auto accident so seriously disfigured, impaired, or scarred that they have scarcely been able to put their lives back together. Often the injury has psychological or social dimensions, as with battered wives and abused children, whose self-image is so badly bruised that they find it difficult to believe in themselves, establish an identity, or develop intimate relationships. We also speak of reputations being damaged, an injury that can readily lead to suicide, as it did recently with Pennsylvania state treasurer, Robert Budd Dwyer. We could expand the category further to include economic injury and legal injury. Each of these forms of injury can constitute a significant threat to a person's integrity or wholeness.

The third and largest category of events that threaten one's being is *loss.* A pitcher who loses his arm, a sculptor who loses her hands, a musician who loses his fingers is likely to feel, "My life is over." Probably most of us would feel that way if faced with loss of sight or hearing or speech. I watched my father, a university professor, slip ever deeper into depression as he lost his mental abilities, one after another, to onrushing senility. Month after month his repeated question was, "What are my prospects?" Losses of such magnitude leave wounds so gaping that it is difficult to reassemble life's remaining pieces in any meaningful way.

Loss of a friend or relative is scarcely easier. "I have lost my right arm!" General Lee exclaimed when informed of the death of Stonewall Jackson. It would be easier for many of us to give up an arm than lose a spouse or a child. Persons married for a lifetime can be so devastated by bereavement that the survivor soon follows his or her spouse to the grave, or continues living only in memories. Grief is hard work, carried on in hope that eventually the broken pieces will grow back together and zest for living will return, yet constantly dogged by the fear that all is lost and life no longer worth living. Divorce can be even more difficult, for there is no decisive "good-bye" equivalent to the closing of the casket.

In the decade of the eighties we have heard a lot about farm foreclosures. Consider the multiple deprivations that they entail. There is, first of all, the loss of a home. My parents, when ill-health forced them to leave the house that they had built thirty-five years earlier, said it was like losing their best friend. How much more bereft is the farm family evicted from the homestead built by immigrant ancestors and identified with the family for generations. There is, in addition, the loss of livelihood, or rather, of a *calling,* for who would endure the rigors of farming, were the soil not in their blood? Even more, there is the loss of a whole way of life, with its unique freedoms and values, unlike any other lifestyle in America, handed down from parents to children, generation after generation. All that, gone. Is there life after the farm for such persons? No wonder so many take their own lives.

Yet there are stories of loss even more woeful — the millions of homeless crowded into the world's cities, and the millions more refugees, who have lost language, nation, and culture, as well as land, home, and often family.

The common thread running through all of these losses — and even through the prior categories of pain and injury — is the *loss of meaning.* Each of us has some configuration of values that makes life worthwhile for us and gives us personal worth. Take away a key value in that configuration, and the result is emptiness, a feeling of hollowness at the core. Existence has lost its purpose, and it feels pointless to go on. That's how Frederick Beaudoin must have felt when he discovered that his entire family had been wiped out and their home burned to the ground. The one thing without which life cannot go on is purpose. If that disappears, then the only thing to keep us going is sheer hope — hope that the wound will heal, the void be filled, and that some new purpose will make life meaningful once again.

This is the language of *transcendence,* the framework of ultimate meaning within which every event and aspect of life finds its significant place. "Everyone has a transcendent dimension, a life of the spirit," Cassell insists — a dimension which, he claims, has been too often neglected by the medical profession. The life of the spirit "is most directly expressed in religion and the mystic traditions," he states, but "anything larger and more enduring than the person is evidence of the universality of the transcendent dimension."[12] In the case of Father Donnelly, the threat to the transcendent source of meaning was quite evident. In such a situation one must either discover a way to ward off that threat, or else face the agony of finding a new basis for life's meaning. This is why for any religious person the conceptual task of reconciling human suffering with foundational faith in God is more than an intellectual exercise. We shall return to that task in the next chapter.

Oppression

Pain, injury, loss — these are the three types of suffering mentioned by Cassell and included in most dictionary definitions of suffering. If we are to expand our horizon beyond the limits of white, middle-class U.S.A., however, then we must add a fourth type of suffering: *oppression.* By oppression I mean the use of cruel or unjust power to suppress or tyrannize a people through violence, intimidation, ideology, or other means. Whether it is racial oppression in South Africa, political tyranny in Afghanistan, genocide in Cambodia, or torture in Chile, all these forms of oppression place in jeopardy not only the existence and worth of individual persons but of whole classes of people. Thus suffering can be corporate as well as individual. Indeed, it is the suffering of the people that is of special concern to the biblical God: "I have seen the affliction of my people who are in Egypt, and have heard their cry" (Exod. 3:7).

Although oppression is a form of suffering all too familiar in the Third World, it is beyond the purview of most people in the United States. I therefore offer an extended illustration, drawn from the eyewitness account of Yvonne Dilling, who in 1981–82 kept a diary of her experience as a volunteer working with Salvadoran refugees in Honduras.[13]

Early on the morning of March 18, 1981, refugees began crossing from El Salvador into Honduras near the tiny Honduran hamlet of Los Hernández. Yvonne and two other refugee workers hastened to the border, where they found a thousand refugees, unable to cross the swift-flowing Lempa River. Quickly they stretched a rope across the fifty-meter wide river to keep refugees from being swept downstream in the current. Yvonne, a strong swimmer, began ferrying children across on her back.

During the several hours of the crossing, a helicopter gunship twice flew low over the river, peppering both banks with machine-gun fire. Yvonne watched petrified as a young boy was gunned down in the water and an old woman, huddled under

the same tree with Yvonne, died with an infant in her arms.
Yvonne could see the gunner's eyes, so she was sure that he
knew his targets were mostly women and children. At dusk the
three refugee workers escorted their charges to Los Hernández.
En route they stumbled across the bodies of two refugees who
had been killed along the trail.

Arriving at nightfall, they found three thousand exhausted
refugees surrounded by Honduran soldiers, who called it a "guerrilla camp." Outside the cordoned area Yvonne could hear the
plaintive cries of children lost in the dark. After laboring all
night among the sick and wounded, a French medical team reported that the most critical health risks were dehydration, mal-
nutrition, and epidemic disease. During the ensuing months
children died daily from diarrhea and dehydration, as anxious
mothers asked themselves, "Will my child be next?"

As the days wore on, the refugees began sharing their stories.
A young woman told Yvonne how government troops had terror-
ized her village. Entering the village one day, they forced open
doors, smashed furniture and dishes, set clothing and bedding
on fire, shot livestock, and uprooted gardens. Three soldiers
burst into her house while her husband was out working in the
fields. One pressed his rifle butt against her throat and another
pinned the children to the wall, while the third soldier searched
the house. When he found a Bible, he demanded, "Admit this is
your Bible. Admit you hide communist literature in it. Admit
you discuss communist takeovers in your so-called Bible study
group." When she denied the accusations, they threatened to
"make her a whore in front of the kids." They left without carrying out their threat, but when soldiers returned a few weeks
later, the family fled.

All the refugees had similar stories. They reported that the
most common accusations brought against them were listening
to Archbishop Romero's sermons, participating in Bible study,
belonging to a union, and the blanket indictment of being "sub-
versive." Many had not escaped as unscathed as the family
described above.

Eventually the U.N. negotiated resettlement to a camp built
a few miles inland from the border, near the town of La Virtud.
Military harassment continued, however, escalating into arrests,
disappearances, torture, and brutal slayings. The nadir was
reached one day in November, when a contingent of Salvadoran

soldiers and plainclothes agents from the dreaded "death squad" crossed the Lempa and raided the camp, dragging off thirty men, women, and children with their thumbs tied behind their backs. A group of international journalists, in the area to report on the refugee situation, pursued with cameras and shouted, "We are taking your pictures. Tomorrow the whole world will know the crime you have committed. Let the people go!" When the startled soldiers grasped the implications of that, they released their prisoners.

Their triumph was short-lived, for soon thereafter the refugees were removed to Mesa Grande, a larger camp in unfamiliar terrain, far from their Salvadoran homes. During the transition the camp director, a Catholic lay pastor supposedly under U.N. protection, was abducted by Honduran soldiers and severely tortured. Only chance discovery by a priest saved him from joining the ranks of the "disappeared."

The story has a sequel. In the fall of 1987, several thousand refugees returned from Mesa Grande and resettled in El Salvador, with the reluctant permission of the Duarte government. The outcome of that bold move is still in doubt, however, as the resettled Salvadorans continue to endure harassment by their own military forces.

In this story we find harassment, humiliation, powerlessness, disruption, torture, and murder — daily experiences of oppression found in much of the Third World. And we find these afflictions laid on top of our First World experiences of pain, injury, and loss, which in that setting are further aggravated by poverty, disease, and powerlessness. If we omitted oppression from our types of suffering, our inventory would miss much of the affliction visited on the majority population of our globe.

We are now ready to return to Cassell's definition and expand it by adding the four categories we have been discussing. *Suffering,* then, *is a state of severe distress occurring when a person or people perceive their intactness or wholeness to be endangered by pain, injury, loss, or oppression.*

Suffering and Soul-making

Earlier we noted that despite important distinctions in meaning, "pain" and "suffering" are often treated as synonyms. Similarly, "suffering" and "evil" are frequently used interchangeably. Such synonymic use implies that suffering is always negative in value, an experience that inescapably diminishes human existence. But is suffering all bad? Is it always a net loss, or is it sometimes the occasion for real growth, resulting in a net gain? And if it is the case that tribulation sometimes turns out to be for the good, might it not be true that over the long haul all suffering actually enhances human life? This is an important theological issue, for if, in the end, all suffering turns out to be for the good, then there is no real evil, and consequently no problem of evil. The belief that *some things should not be* is the necessary presupposition of the "why" question.

So we must ask, is suffering ever actually *good?* Certainly any event that fits Cassell's definition is a terrible experience, but does it ever turn out to enhance the life of the sufferer, or human life generally? Consider the classics of world literature. Many of them are inconceivable apart from the saga of human affliction. Would we go wide of the mark if we said that most of the world's great art has grown out of the personal travail of its creators? Think of Beethoven and Van Gogh and Sylvia Plath. We even say that a work of art lacking the tragic dimension is "shallow." Isn't it, in fact, the case that the heroes we most admire are those who have risen above great adversity and transformed that adversity into virtue? It almost seems that we grow into our full humanity only by confronting sharp challenges and rising above them. Suffering is the stuff out of which wisdom is made. "Call the world if you Please 'The vale of Soul-making,'" John Keats wrote to his brother. "Do you not see how necessary a World of Pains and troubles is to school an Intelligence and make it a Soul?"[14] So suffering is good for you; it is the raw material out of which true humanity is fashioned.

Clearly Keats has a point, but something in us recoils from the generalization that "suffering is good for you." The world has seen too much agony that serves no conceivable redeeming purpose. Would anyone like to propose a redeeming value for Buchenwald, or tell a child terminally ill with leukemia what good is being served by her affliction? Negative experiences often have positive by-products, and some do indeed contribute to a greater good. Yet there are three things about the mass of human suffering that make us refuse to endorse the generalization that suffering is actually beneficial. First, much of it appears *pointless,* contributing little or nothing to human growth. Such suffering is "without redeeming social value," and in that sense, "obscene." Second, most affliction is *unjust*. The wicked prosper while the righteous suffer, as the Psalmist observed millennia ago, and a disproportionately large percentage of the earth's affliction falls on the poor, the marginated, and the oppressed people of this world. Finally, for purposes of "soul-making" it is *excessive*. "Popular theism is refuted by the existence of so much suffering," claims Walter Kaufman, "by Auschwitz and a billion lesser evils."[15] There is far more suffering than is needed to develop nobility, and it comes down so hard on some that it destroys personality instead of building character.

The answer to the question posed, then, is that suffering is not all bad, but neither is it all good. Often good does emerge from suffering, and the ordeal of confronting adversity appears to be an essential ingredient for human growth. Yet in Prospect, Conn., the suffering was pointless, unjust, and excessive. It is such gratuitous suffering that triggers the "why" question, to be addressed in the next chapter.

Suffering and the Quest for Meaning

There is one further uniquely human aspect of suffering that needs to be addressed, namely, its relation to religious faith. To begin with, the very way in which we perceive a traumatic event will depend on the perspective, religious or otherwise, which we bring to that event. This is an important insight of cognitive therapy. What is distressingly threatening to one individual may not be to another, and the difference often lies in the attitude that a person brings to that experience. Because religion is a basic shaper of attitudes and dispositions, faith will profoundly inform the way we perceive and respond to affliction.

A few years ago I met a woman in the hospital whom I shall call Dolores. She had gone through an incredible amount of illness in her thirty-one years of life, including six cardiac arrests and a heart valve implantation. At the time I met her, she was facing cardiac surgery for the second time. Her perspective on this was, "God is testing me." This implied that all her health problems were divinely inflicted by a God who had absolute control over the events in her life. Believing that God was totally in control seemed to provide her with a small bit of security in a very threatening world, even though that security was conditional upon her passing the "test." It was clearly a viewpoint she had learned previously and brought *to* the event.

By contrast, in a nearby church a man came up after each class I was teaching to ask, "When are you going to tell them the important thing? When are you going to tell them that Christ will heal all illness?" You can imagine that this man would approach heart surgery quite differently from Dolores. So the nature of our beliefs and the kind of God in which we place our trust will make a big difference in the way we perceive and handle our suffering.

Not only does faith interpret our experiences of suffering, it can be a significant resource for coping with them. A seminarian who was going through a stressful divorce found strength in prayer and meditation, drawing near to the Christ who, he was convinced, understood his agony because Jesus, too, had undergone agony. In the refugee camp in Honduras, people gained power to endure through identification with Christ's sufferings, portrayed in scripture and dramatized in the church's liturgy. The God who walks with us through the valley of the shadow of death, who descends into hell with us, who promises, "Lo, I am with you always," gives us strength to go on even when ours fails. Dr. Cassell writes,

> Transcendence is probably the most powerful way in which one is restored to wholeness after an injury to personhood. When experienced, transcendence locates the person in a far larger landscape. The sufferer is not isolated by pain but is brought closer to a transpersonal source of meaning and to the human community that shares those meanings.[16]

The relationship between experience and faith, however, is a two-way street. If religious attitude shapes experience, experience also dismantles and rebuilds faith. German theologian Dorothee Sölle states,

> Every suffering that is experienced as a threat to one's own life touches our relationship to God, if we use this expression in the strict theological sense . . . , as something everyone possesses, as that "which a person trusts" (Luther). This (nonexplicit) relationship to God is called into ques-

tion in extreme suffering. The ground on which life was built, the primal trust in the world's reliability...is destroyed.[17]

This means that suffering will almost inevitably involve a reappraisal, sometimes agonizing, of one's whole faith-stance. Kushner himself is a prime example. The faith that he brought to the crisis of his son's death crumbled in the face of that shock. Out of the wreckage, a new and stronger faith was built. The reconstruction process resulted in a new person, a new faith, and a new way of looking at suffering and evil.

A true story of life and death on Mt. Washington illustrates much of what we have been discussing. In 1981 two young men from eastern Pennsylvania, Jeff Batzer and Hugh Herr, got lost in a blizzard while climbing Mt. Washington. Miraculously they were rescued after four days in the snow, but only after one rescuer had lost his life in an avalanche. A months-long struggle to stave off the after-effects of frostbite ensued, but ultimately Hugh lost both legs below the knees, while Jeff lost his left leg below the knee plus the fingers and toes of his right hand and foot. Recuperation was slow, with many discouraging setbacks; yet within two years Hugh was back mountain-climbing on artificial legs, and Jeff was participating in a bicycle race up Mt. Washington, the very site of his catastrophe. Hugh, frequently shown mountain-climbing on television, is today considered one of the premier mountain-climbers in the country. He loves talking about mountain-climbing, but he won't discuss the incident on Mt. Washington, explaining that he wants to put that behind him. The most he will say is, "This stuff happens. Climbers die all the time, but everything is dangerous." In other words, life is risky and accidents will happen.

By contrast, Jeff frequently talks to scout groups about safety, bringing along the very clothing and gear he used on that disastrous climb. He also speaks to church groups about the incident and how he has grown as a result of it. He talks of his feelings and fears during those days on the mountain. Then he tells his audience that his life has been rebuilt much better than before, that the horrifying experience has helped him grow closer to his family, his world, and his God. He is convinced that the incident on the mountain was all part of God's grand design. "I was a Christian before the accident," he says, "but it has given me a deeper understanding of God." He adds that he wouldn't be where he is today without the trials he has faced, and he wouldn't change that. He views this new insight into life as a gift from God, a gift he is "now trying to pass on to others who have yet to come face to face with their own mortality." The experience has changed him, his friends claim, from a shy word-stumbler to a secure, eloquent speaker.

He says that his attitudes have changed, too. Instead of competing with others, he now finds satisfaction in setting himself goals and achieving them. He still retains an unusual love for the mountain. "I look at it almost like a friend," he says. "It pushed me to the end of my existence...and let me live. I love it for that." What troubles him most is the volunteer who lost his life trying to rescue him. "The last thing I ever wanted to do was to have somebody die because of me."[18]

Here are two young men who brought to this accident a huge love of life and adventure and a desire to push themselves to the limit in order to test what they could do. They knew there were dangers involved in that, and they were willing to take the risk. Jeff brought his religious faith to the mountain with him, and interpreted his ordeal in light of that belief. His faith was clearly tempered by that experience: he states that he came face to face with his own mortality. Yet if his religious belief was shaken, he doesn't say so. As a result of the experience Jeff has grown, his faith has deepened, his life is "better than before," and he wouldn't change any of it. For Jeff Batzer, those four days of horror have turned out for the good. The one piece that still doesn't fit into that interpretation is the death of his rescuer.

Hugh is also a Christian, a member of an Evangelical Free church, but how his faith related to the ordeal, and whether it was shaken or strengthened, he doesn't say. His mode of coping, apparently, is to seal off the horror. While Jeff dwells on the intimate details, Hugh wants to push the event out of his mind.

Jeff's and Hugh's stories are offered not as models of faith, but as illustrations of the way in which religious faith is intimately involved in suffering. Religious belief shapes the perspective we bring to suffering, it is tempered and sometimes shattered by suffering, and it can be a creative resource for putting life back together. Jeff and Hugh's story is also a fine illustration of the way in which two seemingly similar persons respond differently to the same traumatic event.

Chapter 2

"Why, God?":
Omnipotence Reconsidered

In the last chapter we examined the multiple murders in Prospect, Conn., as a case study in suffering, promising to return in this chapter to Father Donnelly's questions, "How could something like this happen? Why does God let this go on? Why do the innocent suffer?" Those questions, ancient as Job, are virtually a reflex response to senseless suffering. It is the age-old issue of theodicy, of justifying God's ways.[1]

The tragic episode in Prospect was for Father Donnelly a pointless horror. To have suggested some just purpose for it would have seemed obscene. We have a word for such horrors, and Father Donnelly used it: "There is evil in the world." To call something "evil" says more than that it is painful or distressing. "Evil" implies a negative value-judgment. We call what happens "evil" if it diminishes or obliterates value or prevents the attainment of good. Evil is destructive; it's a waste. Better that it never happened!

Identifying a catastrophic event as evil, however, does not automatically implicate God. To ask why *God* lets this go on makes sense only if we believe that God has power to prevent it. And indeed, that is what one would expect Father Donnelly to believe, for church doctrine has traditionally taught that God is *omnipotent,* the all-powerful creator and sovereign ruler of all. "With God all things are possible," Jesus says (Matt. 19:26). "Are not two sparrows sold for a penny? And not one of them will fall to the ground without your Father's will?" (Matt. 10:19).

Omnipotence is written into the first article of the Apostles' Creed: "I believe in God the Father *almighty.*" A more accurate rendering of the original Greek term, *pantokrator,* would be "Ruler of All," and that brings out an important nuance of omnipotence: God's sovereignty. Today's bumper sticker puts it succinctly: "God is in control." Omnipotence, then, is an essential divine attribute for orthodox faith. The dictionary defines omnipotence as "having unlimited power."[2] In everyday speech it means, "God can accomplish whatever God wills," or "There are no limits to what God can do," or "Nothing happens without divine permission." If that is the proper definition of divine omnipotence, then it was easily within God's power to prevent the multiple murder of the Beaudoin family.

Yet it is conceivable that an omnipotent being might have such power but not use it to prevent evil. Perhaps God is indifferent to the human condition. "Wake up, Lord! Why are you asleep?" the psalmist cries (Ps. 49:23, TEV), as if God's interest needed to be aroused. Or even worse, perhaps God is sadistic, taking pleasure in the hurts of humans. Either way, the tragedy in Prospect would pose no theological problem, for what else would one expect from a callous or cruel sovereign? To question, "Why do the innocent suffer?" makes sense only because Father Donnelly believes in a God of unlimited goodness as well as unlimited power, a God who genuinely cares about us and exercises an even-handed justice incompatible with destruction of the innocent. The attribute of divine goodness is so basic a tenet of the Judeo-Christian tradition that most believers would regard it as intrinsic to the very meaning of deity. A God who is not good simply isn't God. Thus omnipotence and perfect goodness are commonly linked as the two essential divine attributes. "By definition," says Leander Keck, "God is...the Holy One, that is, the One in Whom integrity and power coincide."[3]

The assertion of divine goodness brings God into direct relation with evil, for "good" and "evil" have meaning only by contrast with each other. "The meaning of evil cannot be understood apart from its relation to good," states S. Paul Schilling. "Normatively, *good* refers to experiences that are really desirable because they enrich and fulfill life, while *evil* refers to those that thwart such fulfilment and impede the actualization of value."[4] Given this polar contrast, one may legitimately expect that a good being will always oppose evil. Ethicist Philip Hallie defines evil simply as "doing harm," and states, "To be against evil is to be against the destruction of human life and against the passions that motivate that destruction."[5] A God of perfect goodness will thus seek to prevent or eliminate those things that destroy human life or thwart human fulfilment.

The problem of evil, then, is produced by the inconsistency that we feel among the three basic claims we have been examining: (1) God is omnipotent, (2) God is perfectly good, (3) there is evil in the world. Intuitively we sense that all three cannot be true together. Unless the appearance of evil in the world is only an illusion, either God wills to prevent evil but cannot, in which case God is not all-powerful, or else God can prevent it but will not, in which case God is not perfectly good. The quandary is well-expressed by Nickles in Archibald MacLeish's play, *J.B.*:

> If God is God He is not good,
> If God is good He is not God.[6]

But if, as we have been arguing, the very meaning of the word "God" requires *both* omnipotence and perfect goodness, then we are faced with an unhappy forced choice: either evil is not real, or such a God does not exist. The existence of evil has become an argument for atheism, and many have found it a persuasive argument.

The believer, however, will seek some other solution to the problem. In logic, if the conclusion of an argument is unacceptable, then the only recourse is to attack the premises, either *rejecting* one of them outright, or *revising* one of them so that the contradiction disappears. Here that means rejecting or revising one of the three premises identified above, which, for convenience, we may label as (1) omnipotence, (2) benevolence, (3) evil. The believer's dilemma is actually a "tri-lemma," for one of the three "lemmas" (assumptions) must be relinquished.

Father Donnelly cannot gloss over the evil in the situation, but neither can he forsake the almighty and loving God. He feels the logical bind, not just in his head, but in the pit of his stomach. It is important to recognize that the problem of evil is not some armchair philosopher's teaser, but challenges a person's whole being. There is an existential logic — a "logic of the gut," if you will — which brings radical doubt to forceful emotional expression in crisis. That logic is driven by the irrepressible quest to make sense out of life's seeming contradictions, combined with a primordial conviction that life ought to be fair and that God should be the Guarantor of that fairness.

That irrepressible existential logic led young Elie Wiesel to

parody the Rosh Hashanah prayer in Buna: "Blessed art Thou,
Eternal, Master of the Universe, Who chose us from among
the races to be tortured day and night, ... to be butchered on
Thine altar."[7] We see it operating again when Karen Quinlan's
brother John shouted in outrage to his mother, "How can you
still believe in God?"[8]

Father Donnelly, unable to wriggle out of the bind he feels
among those three basic convictions, falls back on *mystery.* "We
have all found that there are no answers — none at all." A little
further into his homily, however, he does venture an answer: "It
is an evil that man inflicts on himself and his world whenever
he fails to respect God, himself or his fellow man." The evil, in
other words, is to be laid at the feet of human beings, not God.
That might seem like a way out of the quandary, and indeed, *free
choice* is the most frequently employed response to the problem
of evil. The logical problem is not so easily escaped, however,
for if omnipotence means that God can accomplish *anything,*
then God could have intervened to prevent the dastardly deed.
Father Donnelly's answer in effect limits divine power. Humans,
he asserts, have the capacity to act out of respect or disrespect
for God, self, and others. As long as God honors that human
freedom to act, there are some things God cannot do. Father
Donnelly's answer amounts to either a rejection of omnipotence
or an attenuation of its meaning. It is a fair assumption that he
intends the latter.

Before examining in greater detail this and other responses to
the riddle of evil, let us compare the story from Prospect, Conn.,
to a similar news item from Hillsdale, N.J., that appeared just
two months later.

"God Planned This Accident"

More than 600 friends and relatives of five "born-again"
Christian teen-agers killed in a traffic accident gave thanks
at a funeral service Wednesday that the youths "are now
with Jesus."

Parishioners and church leaders said they believe the
deaths were part of God's plan and added that they hope to
find strength in their faith from the tragedy, which occurred
as the teen-agers were returning home after a day of Bible
study.

"Buckets of tears have been shed," said the Rev. Fred Beveridge, pastor of the Pascack Bible Church. "The pain of our hearts is like a knife, but behind this is the confidence in Jesus Christ."

Maria Van Beers, 15, of Upper Saddle River, N.J.; Brian Hayhurst, 17; his brother, Mark, 15; Eric Borloz, 15; and Thomas E. Carroll, 14; all of Westwood, N.J., were killed Saturday night when the van in which they were riding collided with another van. Also killed were the driver of the second vehicle, Stuart Stricklett, 28, of Allendale, N.J., and his brother, Roger, 26, of Waldwick, N.J.

Police said Stricklett was speeding and attempted to pass another car when the accident occurred.

"We know that God had planned this accident that way," a member of the church's youth group said at the funeral. "He had them prepared for it and, in a short while, they will be with him."

Walter Van Beers, Maria's father, noted that the teenagers were different than most of their peers.

"They weren't popular in the way of the world," he told the congregation while looking at the five flower-covered coffins. "They turned away from alcohol. They turned away from drugs. They turned away from wild parties and promiscuity and anything not pleasing to God."

Van Beers, his voice breaking at times, urged the parishioners to pray for the Stricklett brothers. "We hold no bitterness in our hearts for our brothers who caused this accident," he said. . . .

Classmates of the five youths echoed the sentiments of their elders that there must have been a purpose in the deaths.[9]

Once again we are confronted with the deaths of a group of apparently innocent victims, and again the anguish of the survivors is intense. "Buckets of tears have been shed," the pastor says. "The pain of our hearts is like a knife." The suffering in Hillsdale is as real as that in Prospect. Yet here there are no agonizing questions like those of Father Donnelly — at least, not on the surface.[10] The reason is that the survivors are confident that a good God was completely in control of the whole event. "We know that God had planned this accident that way," says one of the speakers. "He had them prepared for it." The divine sovereignty here is total, even including the manner in which it happened.

The word "evil" never appears in this news account, and for good reason. If a good God planned the accident, then it could not be evil. There is no riddle of evil for the persons at this funeral because they find no evil in the situation. The evil is only *apparent,* not *actual.* Rejecting the assumption of evil eliminates the contradiction. The solution is purchased at the price of denying not only evil, however, but also human freedom, for if God "planned this accident that way," then it was no "accident," and no human action could have changed the outcome.

That is certainly one way to elucidate the remarks made at the funeral in Hillsdale. Yet the denial of human freedom is inconsistent with Walter Van Beers's claim that these born-again Christians were different. "They turned away from alcohol...drugs... promiscuity and anything not pleasing to God." Furthermore, he asserts that the Stricklett brothers "caused this accident." The implication is that both sets of young people were free to choose their course of action — free to choose good or evil. Even if that is what Van Beers means, he still will not allow that any human action could frustrate the ultimate purpose of God, who used apparently evil deeds to achieve a greater good in the indefeasible perfection of the divine plan.

This second interpretation finds a "greater good" argument in the remarks of Van Beers and others at the funeral. Whereas the first interpretation solved the problem by denying that in this situation there is any evil (third premise), the second interpretation amounts to a redefinition of benevolence (second premise): God triumphs over evil not by preventing it, but by turning it into good. Such "greater good" arguments will be found in many of the answers that have been given to the riddle of evil.[11] It is often difficult to distinguish between a response denying evil and one claiming that evil is being used to achieve a greater good.

Another important observation from this case is that evil is not a fact to be read directly from the data, but an interpretation of the data, about which observers may disagree. One person may see the fatal automobile crash as a horrible loss, incompatible with any good purpose, while another will view it positively as one more event unfolding from the amazing providence of God. Even the same person may see things differently at different times. What at first appears to be evil, therefore, may actually be good when viewed in the "right" perspective. This is the heart of the theological response to tragedy in the Pascack Bible Church: what from a worldly perspective appears evil, from the larger perspective of divine providence is known to be good. As we consider the problem of evil, then, we must bear in mind both the *perspective* of the interpreter and the distinction between *apparent* evil and actual evil.[12]

Theological Responses

We have now examined both the logical structure and the emotional force of the riddle of evil. Our two cases have also put forward several alternative answers to that predicament. These answers are, in fact, representative of the possible responses that can be made in order to escape the atheistic conclusion. Basically, three types of responses are possible, corresponding to our three premises, and there are two variants of each type. One may either *reject* one of the three premises outright, or else *redefine* its key term. These, then, are the formal possibilities:

1. *Responses rejecting or redefining divine omnipotence.* The responses in this category all claim that God is not solely responsible for everything that happens. In addition to God, there are other powers that determine the outcome of events, and it is these other powers — divine, angelic, human, or natural — that bring evil into the world. These other powers constitute a limitation on God's power, contradicting the dictionary definition of omnipotence as "having unlimited power." Omnipotence, then, must either be rejected or else redefined in such a way as to make room for other powers. Father Donnelly, in identifying *human* decisions as the source of evil, was either denying omnipotence or significantly qualifying its popular meaning.

2. *Responses rejecting or redefining divine benevolence.* Elie Wiesel's satirical Rosh Hashanah amounted to an outright rejection of God's goodness. By contrast, the remarks of Walter Van Beers (according to our second interpretation) imply a definition of benevolence in which divine goodness permits some evil in order to bring about a greater good.

3. *Responses rejecting or redefining evil.* "God planned the

accident" sounds like a denial that there is any genuine evil at all in that situation. Even if it is claimed that the evil was transformed into good, we have to wonder whether evil has not lost its "evilness" in the process.[13]

If we look at the actual answers to evil that have been given by religious people across the centuries, testifying out of their personal situations of anguish, we can identify ten specific responses, all of which fall under one or another of these three basic types. Should all ten of those answers prove unsatisfactory, then only two further options remain: accept atheism or plead mystery.

Altogether, then, there are twelve possible responses, summarized in the table on p. 25. In the remainder of this chapter we shall explore the four responses that reject or redefine omnipotence. In the following chapter we will examine the remaining options and draw some conclusions.

Responses Rejecting or Redefining Omnipotence

The responses in our first category all acknowledge some limitation on divine power. First, however, it is important to mention one "limit" on God's power that is accepted by virtually all philosophers and theologians: God cannot do what is logically impossible. "Logical impossibility" refers to self-contradictions. "Round square" is the commonly-cited illustration. In that pair of words, the definition of each term excludes the other, so that combining those words yields nonsense. Were someone to persist in claiming, "Nevertheless, a truly omnipotent God could create a round square," it would be evident that this person didn't understand the meaning of the words. It would be similar nonsense to insist that God could create flat spheres or married bachelors, or could bring it about that Kennedy was assassinated and died of old age. It does not reduce God's power one iota to assert that God cannot perform such nonsense.

This may seem a trivial point, but it assumes enormous significance when, on the grounds of logical impossibility, it is claimed that even an omnipotent God "can't give these creatures the freedom to perform evil and at the same time prevent them from doing so" (Alvin Plantinga),[14] or that "not even Omnipotence could create a society of free souls without at the same time creating a relatively independent and 'inexorable'

TWELVE THEOLOGICAL RESPONSES
TO THE PROBLEM OF EVIL

Positions Rejecting or Redefining Omnipotence

1. *Dualism.* There is a perpetual struggle between two ultimate forces, the power of good against the power of evil, and the latter is the cause of the ills we suffer.

2. *Satan.* Within God's good creation there is a domain of evil powers (Satan and the demons) who are "fallen" from an original angelic status and who insinuate evil into the world.

3. *Natural Order.* Suffering is the unavoidable by-product of natural forces and rhythms operating in an ordered universe, which is God's good creation.

4. *Free Choice.* Finite creatures endowed by their Creator with freedom have the capacity to make bad choices, resulting in evil consequences. *Sub-types:* (a) error, (b) sin, (c) fallenness (original sin), (d) structures of evil.

Positions Rejecting or Redefining the Goodness of God

5. *Despotism.* Evil is either permitted or willed by God because in relation to other beings God is indifferent or unjust or malicious.

6. *Judgment.* Suffering is God's retributive or corrective judgment on our sinful ways.

7. *Testing.* Affliction is a God-given ordeal to put our faith to the test.

8. *Personal Growth.* To achieve maturity, persons need to overcome hardship, anguish, and defeat.

Positions Denying or Redefining Evil

9. *Illusion.* The ills we seem to suffer are actually illusory, the result of erroneous thinking.

10. *Partial Perspective.* Although the evils we experience are real, if they could be viewed from a more inclusive perspective, they would be seen to contribute to a larger, harmonious whole.

Additional Positions

11. *Atheism.* The reality of evil in the world makes belief in God impossible.

12. *Mystery.* A problem such as this, involving the power and purpose of the infinite God, is beyond the capacity of finite minds to solve.

Nature" (C. S. Lewis).[15] These two claims, grounded in logical necessity, form the bases for responses three and four below.

All the responses in this category trace the source of evil to powers in the universe other than God, powers that place limitations on what God can do. If beings other than God exist with some power to influence events, then God does not possess *all* power (even if, in some primordial past, God as creator was the only power). If it is true that God does not hold a monopoly of power, then there are limits to what God can do, and we shall have to abandon the traditional notion of omnipotence in favor of a God whose power is to some degree limited by other beings. An alternative, of course, is to redefine omnipotence so that it is compatible with the existence of other beings having limited powers of their own. Perhaps what "omnipotence" really means is that God is the sole source of all power, some of which the creator has delegated to creatures, as the biblical notion of "dominion" implies (Gen. 1:28). Or perhaps "omnipotence" means "omnicompetence" or "all-sufficiency," that is, God's ability to achieve the divine purpose even while sharing power with other beings.[16]

In the following four positions, the power-other-than-God that is the source of evil is (1) another uncreated, ultimate being (such as an opposing, evil God), or (2) a supernatural creature (such as Satan), or (3) the created world of nature, or (4) creatures in the world who possess freedom to choose for or against God.

Response One: Dualism

There is a perpetual struggle between two ultimate forces, the power of good against the power of evil, and the latter is the cause of the ills we suffer.

Sometimes human experience makes it seem that there are forces of good and evil locked in deadly combat and that the power of evil is so strong that it cannot be vanquished. At such times dualism seems persuasive, and we draw upon the images of battle to express that struggle. Consider the dramatic duels in which the evil figure always returns to fight another day: Sherlock Holmes against Moriarty, Batman against Joker, Luke Skywalker against Darth Vader. Dualism also has a certain aesthetic appeal, parallel to the cosmic symmetry between matter and anti-matter postulated by physicists.[17]

The classic religious expression of this position is Zoroastrianism, with its eternal struggle between the good god Ormazd and the evil god Ahriman, two equally primordial deities contending for control of the world. Such dualism is foreign to the Hebrew Bible, with its emphasis on the One God who is sole source of all, but the disastrous history of Israel after the Babylonian captivity made Judaism, and subsequently Christianity, open to a modified dualism in the person of Satan (see Response Two below).

A somewhat different dualism, even more ancient, is the mythic struggle of the Creator to overcome chaos. Here again we have two equally primal principles. In the Babylonian creation myth, the creator-god Marduk goes forth to battle against the rebellious forces of chaos (evil), symbolized by the sea-monster/goddess Tiamat. In a fierce struggle, Marduk slays Tiamat. Cutting her watery carcass in two, he fashions a universe between the heavenly waters above and the watery abyss beneath. The triumph of order over the threatening power of chaos is never finally complete, however, for chaos is constantly threatening to break out anew, bringing into the world all the evils we fear. Here the myth surely strikes a universal chord, giving expression to the endemic fear that things are falling apart and that order is imperiled by chaos. Consequently every new year in ancient Babylon, as the waters of the Tigris and Euphrates rose to flood-stage, the drama was ritually re-enacted in order to establish control once again. This concern for order spawned a Babylonian version of civil religion, for part of Marduk's work of ordering the chaos was the establishment of a state, whose king was vested with divine authority to uphold order.

Vestiges of this Babylonian story can be found in the symbolism of water and the step-by-step ordering of creation in Genesis 1, and in the figure of the serpent in Genesis 2. Such a "theogonic myth"[18] did not find favor in Western theology, however, because it compromised the sole sovereignty of God by postulating chaos as coeternal with God. As a defense, the church promulgated the doctrine of *creatio ex nihilo* (creation out of nothing) in order to reject any implied dualism of creator and creation: God alone is ultimate and eternal.

Yet the myth of cosmic struggle against chaos continues to

speak to the human condition, even in our own age. After experiencing the maelstrom of evil that broke loose in mid-century, theologian Edwin Lewis became convinced that so much evil could not be attributed solely to human misbehavior. "It goes down to the very roots of existence," he insisted. The Creator and the Adversary — "the discreative demonic" — were from the beginning locked in conflict.[19]

Harold Kushner also drew upon this ancient myth to make sense of his own personal experience when his son was diagnosed as suffering from progeria, a rare and fatal birth defect afflicting no more than a dozen persons worldwide. Unable to find any theologically satisfying explanation among the traditional responses, Kushner attributed his son's fatal genetic defect to a random remnant of the chaos, which God has not yet brought fully under control.[20]

Kushner may well have borrowed from process theologians, although their dualism is a symbiosis of God and the world, rather than the struggle of creation against chaos. There are twin ultimates in this school of thought, for the idea of "creator" is meaningless without "creation." As long as there has been a creator, there must also have been a creation. Process thinking views creation as an unending process, with a multiplicity of entities constantly coming into being and perishing. Evil arises not from the world as such, but from the inevitable conflict among the actual entities in the world, each of which is partially self-determining. Just as in a society individuals with competing aims inescapably collide with each other, so individuals in the cosmic society inevitably clash, resulting in pain and loss. In process thinking, the fact that from the beginning God shares power in a pluralistic world makes evil virtually inescapable.[21]

Response Two: Satan

Within God's good creation there is a domain of evil powers (Satan and the demons) who are "fallen" from an original angelic status and who insinuate evil into the world.

Satan has enjoyed a long career, but it began late in biblical history. In the older strata of the Hebrew Bible, God alone is the source of both good and evil. In Isaiah we read, "I make weal and create woe, I am the Lord, who do all these things"

(Isa. 45:7). Amos asks, "Does evil befall a city, unless the Lord has done it?" (Amos 3:6). When Saul hurls a spear at David while the latter is playing the lyre, the Bible says that "an evil spirit from God rushed upon Saul" (1 Sam. 18:10). Over time, however, the inner contradiction of a God of justice who causes evil became too great, and evil came to be attributed to other sources, including Satan.

Yet Satan as a personal being appears only three times in Hebrew texts. "Satan" as a noun, meaning "adversary" or "one who stands in the way," is used more often, usually in relation to humans, but sometimes even to describe God (Num. 22:31). In the three passages where Satan does appear as a character (1 Chron. 21:1, Job 1-2, Zech. 3:1-5), the term is *ha satan* — literally, "the adversary" or "the accuser." It is a title rather than a name. For instance, in Job 1-2 *ha satan* is a member of the heavenly host. He is God's intimate advisor, whose task on earth is to search out human behavior and bring accusations before God. He is a sort of private investigator, prosecuting attorney, and enforcer, all rolled into one. The satan suggests to God a violent test of Job's faith, but here, as elsewhere in the Hebrew Bible, Satan can do only what God authorizes him to do.

The New Testament gives us a very different portrait of Satan. What happened in the intertestamental period was repeated conquest and oppression of the Jewish people, to the point where older explanations of human suffering seemed inadequate to account for the immensity of evil they were experiencing. A more dualistic explanation began to emerge in the Hebrew literature of this period, doubtless influenced by the Persian dualism that was spreading throughout the Middle East.

Satan in the New Testament is synonymous with the Devil, the Evil One, Beelzebub. No longer the title of a servant in the heavenly court, Satan is now the name for the enemy of God. A cosmic struggle for control of the world is taking place, with God and Christ ranged on one side, Satan and the demons on the other. Satan has gained such a strong foothold that St. John calls him "the ruler of this world" (John 12:31; 14:30; 16:11) and St. Paul speaks of him as "the God of this world" (2 Cor. 4:4). Satan's control is frequently exercised through earthly rulers, the "principalities and powers." His grip is also manifest in de-

monic possession, a major cause of illness in the New Testament.
Temptation, above all, is Satan's stock in trade; consequently Jesus teaches his disciples to pray, "Lead us not into temptation, but deliver us from the Evil One" (Matt. 6:13).[22] Satan's hold will not last, however, for Jesus' message is that God's Reign is "at hand" (Mark 1:15). This world under Satan's control is coming to an end.

This drama of cosmic struggle between God and Satan bears considerable resemblance to Zoroastrian dualism, but there are important differences. Unlike the Persian myth, the New Testament gives scant attention to evil's origin, simply recognizing cosmic evil, personalized in the figure of Satan, as very real and powerful in this world. Although this evil is supernatural, Satan is not a deity, co-eternal with God, but merely a creature, an angel of God whose arrogance has led him to rebel against his maker. This account of Satan's origins, assumed rather than stated in the New Testament, bears more resemblance to the Eden story than the Zoroastrian myth. At most, then, Satan represents a modified dualism. Furthermore, traces of the older portrait of Satan as God's servant continue. When Jesus is "led up by the Spirit into the wilderness to be tempted by the devil" (Matt. 4:1), the latter is obviously serving the divine purpose, whether he recognizes it or not.[23]

The strength of this response to the problem of evil is that it postulates a sufficiently powerful source to account for the massive evil in the world without falling into a strict dualism. Other responses seem to minimize evil, or heap excessive blame for it on humankind, or else blame God. The chief weakness of this response is that it seriously compromises divine omnipotence. Even though it maintains the ultimate triumph of God's justice, it offers no satisfactory explanation why that final victory is so long delayed, or why Satan was permitted to secure such a strong grip on creation in the first place. Another drawback is its potential for lifting responsibility from human beings by providing a scapegoat for humanly perpetrated evil.

In the classic versions of our first two responses, dualism and Satan, what happens in the world is attributed almost entirely to supernatural, occult powers. The next two positions are based on quite different assumptions about the forces that shape the natural world and human history.

Response Three: Natural Order

Suffering is the unavoidable by-product of natural forces and rhythms operating in an ordered universe, which is God's good creation.

The patterned structure of the universe is an aspect of its created goodness. Human life as we know it would be inconceivable apart from such reliable order. Without the regular rotation of the earth and the measured radiation of the sun, we would never get to work on time (whatever "time" might mean). Take away the precise accuracy of the laws of motion, and travel would be hazardous, if not impossible. Without the dependability of nature, we would quickly be reduced to gibbering idiocy. Nature's rhythms are a manifestation of the trustworthiness of a covenanting God. "While the earth remains," God vows after the Flood, "seedtime and harvest, cold and heat, summer and winter, day and night, shall not cease" (Gen. 8:22). Bernhard Anderson comments, "Thus the regularities of nature, which modern men have rationalized into 'laws,' are at bottom expressions of the faithfulness of God upon which men rely."[24]

Yet that very order can result in disastrous consequences. The same meteorological forces that create lush Caribbean islands also produce devastating hurricanes. Gravity brings down airplanes. Life is parasitic on life, and new life can arise only where death has cleared space. Indeed, the universe is a single system, so that a change introduced at any point will reverberate throughout the whole. Thus the dynamic order that is an expression of divine trustworthiness also places limits on what God can do. Traditionally that restriction has been regarded as self-imposed: God has limited the divine omnipotence in order that there might be a dependable world in which to live.[25]

That raises the question of miracles, in the sense of events or actions that apparently contradict known scientific laws. Rabbi Kushner says, "Laws of nature do not make exceptions for nice people,"[26] but does the Creator never overrule those divinely created laws? Certainly omnipotence means that God has power to do so, and there are abundant honest witnesses, including biblical ones, who attest that they have received such a miracle. In the face of such testimony, it would be foolhardy to say, "Never."

Yet there are some difficulties to be faced, both empirical and logical. If miraculous healing is possible, one has to wonder why so few receive it out of the millions who earnestly and faithfully seek it, and what sort of justice it is that discriminates among equally worthy candidates. Especially perplexing is Auschwitz. If God can and does on occasion intervene, why not at Auschwitz? Why were the fervent prayers for divine deliverance by those being herded into gas chambers — attested by many survivors — met with divine silence?

A further consideration is that if God does sometimes intervene in the intricate balance of nature and override human responsibility for human affairs, logic suggests that such exceptions to the patterned structure of the world must be rare. If there were frequent divine interruptions of the regularities we depend on, order would soon dissolve into chaos, human accountability would become nonsensical, and the universe would appear to operate according to divine whim. The alternative, once again, is to view miracles in a different way. "Miracle" defined as "a violation of the laws of nature" is, after all, a modern concept that never puzzled biblical writers. In the biblical perspective, a miracle is "a special display of God's power," and the natural world itself is such a display.[27] Perhaps miracles, then, should be viewed as manifestations of divine power working through the ordered structure of the world rather than against it, functioning in ways that we humans do not adequately comprehend. Such an understanding of miracle preserves the continuity between God's wondrous work in all creation and God's special concern for each creature.

A contemporary footnote concludes our consideration of natural order. Within the patterned behavior of the natural world, physics has discovered a measure of randomness or chance. Scientific "laws" are now considered to be statistical averages summarizing patterns of behavior among many random events, no one of which is predictable with more than some degree of probability. The early Einstein, to whom such randomness seemed counterintuitive, resolutely insisted that "God does not play dice," but apparently God does, for today the Principle of Indeterminacy is firmly established. Indeed, without some degree of "play" within the structured determinacies of nature, there would seem to be no space in which free choice (see Response Four below) could operate. This has significant implications for our consideration of theodicy. If randomness is not an illusion, then accidents really do happen, as our ordinary language attests, and this must be included among the reasons why calamity strikes.

Response Four: Free Choice

Finite creatures endowed by their Creator with freedom have the capacity to make bad choices, resulting in evil consequences.

The Bible speaks of humans as created "in the image of God" (Gen. 1:26–27; 9:6; 1 Cor. 11:7; cf. Ps. 8:5). Although this symbol is rich with ambiguity, it has usually been interpreted to include freedom and responsibility to decide among alternative possible actions, each leading to a different consequence. Humans endowed with this capacity have the potential to select options that are destructive, injurious, or oppressive, thereby introducing the possibility of evil.

This position, which in recent years has become known as the "Free-will Defense,"[28] is the classic Christian response to the problem of evil. According to this view, evil is not to be blamed on God, or on an evil deity competing with God, or on Satan (although Satan, himself a free being, may play a role as tempter). Instead, it is humans who, because of their bad choices, bear the major responsibility for evil in the world. In arguing this view, C. S. Lewis estimated that four-fifths of the world's afflictions can be attributed to human wickedness (though how he arrived at that statistic remains a mystery).[29] Even the Holocaust, argues Rabbi Arnold Wolf in opposition to Elie Wiesel, does not constitute an accusation against God, but stands as "a warning about human sin."[30]

This does not mean that humans are inherently evil, however, for that would indict their maker. On the contrary, humans have been created "little less than God," endowed with the capacity to reflect the divine love back to their creator. The ability to respond freely is essential to this, for God intended to create beings who could return the divine love not because, like robots, they must, but because they wish to do so. Yet that desirable quality of free response inevitably carries with it the risk of introducing evil into the world, for a being that is free to choose the better is ipso facto also free to choose the worse. Where many finite, free beings all have the possibility of bad choices, it is virtually inevitable that some evil will be actualized.

That is a high price to pay, the advocates of this position

admit, but the benefit exceeds the cost, for the world would be diminished significantly if it lacked creatures who could freely love God and each other. The Free-will Defense is thus a greater good argument: in spite of the fact that humans have contributed massively to the world's evil, a world including such beings, together with the consequent evil, is better than a world without free beings. Augustine put it this way: "As a runaway horse is better than a stone which does not run away because it lacks self-movement and sense perception, so the creature is more excellent which sins by free will than that which does not sin only because it has no free will."[31]

A frequent rejoinder to this line of reasoning is, "Could not God have created beings who would always freely choose the good?" Although the argument over this issue is complex and continuing, the traditional answer has been "no." The very meanings of the key words "responsible" and "love" require that beings possessing these characteristics always have the ability to do otherwise. "Only a free creature could love," claims Douglas John Hall:

> A being programmed to love would be no lover. A being predetermined to act responsibly within creation would hardly warrant our using the adjective *responsible* in its description. Yet the freedom to love presupposes the freedom not to love, and the freedom to assume responsibility willingly presupposes the freedom to renounce it.[32]

Hall is here demonstrating that the very concept of a being who is both morally free and guaranteed always to make the right choice is self-contradictory, as nonsensical as "round square." But, as previously noted, to create nonsense is just as impossible for God as for anyone else. Consequently, it makes no sense to expect God to create a being who would always freely choose the good.

The existence of a world that includes free beings thus places limits on God and on what God can do. If that world is under stood to be the creation of God alone, then the limitation is God's self-limitation, and God's refusal to take away that freedom is part of God's covenanting faithfulness, as with "natural order." Because freedom to choose is meaningful only in a cause-and-effect world in which outcomes of choices can be anticipated with some reliability, this position presupposes natural order. Also, although it is usually human freedom that is being considered, some theologians, notably those influenced by process philosophy, extend creaturely freedom to subhuman or superhuman levels. Human or otherwise, freedom must be distinguished from randomness, for what we have in mind is not chance accidents, but consequences deliberately selected from among different possible alternatives.

There are four ways in which free choice contributes to evil in the world. Although the four are significantly different from one another, each slips easily into the next without clearly-marked lines of demarcation.

a. *Error.* Creatures are finite in knowledge and skill and therefore capable of making mistakes. Occasionally such an error can have catastrophic consequences. In the findings of the National Transportation Safety Board, the most common cause of airline disasters is "pilot error." The same would surely also be true of highway and rail accidents. Human error as a cause of evil has been underestimated in the literature on theodicy.[33] At the same time, it must be acknowledged that disaster inquiries sometimes indicate something more reprehensible than a mere mistake. Recent findings of drug use by railroad crews are a case in point. Such factors move us in the direction of the second form of this response.

b. *Sin.* A free creature, knowing which option is the better and which the worse, may deliberately choose the worse, perhaps viewing it as better for himself or herself. Greed, exploitation, and oppression are all illustrations. Sin is not the same as a "mistake" or "error," even though the offender might choose to use that euphemism.

Sin is an important biblical category. The frequent scriptural exhortations to "keep the commandments" (Deut. 10:13), to "seek good, and not evil" (Amos 5:14), to "choose life" (Deut. 30:19), all presuppose human freedom to make choices and keep promises. In strictly theological terms, sin is turning away from God toward some lesser good, pridefully preferring one's own perceived good to the divine purpose.

c. *Fallenness (Original Sin).* As we have seen, much of the world's tribulation has been blamed on human choices; but are human decisions really as free as that assumes? Often we feel trapped in bad habits or harmful behaviors or destructive thought-patterns that stubbornly resist our resolve to break their grip. On the level of personal experience we all understand St. Paul's cry, "I do not do the good I want, but the evil I do not want is what I do" (Rom. 7:19). The sinner, says St. John, "is a slave to sin" (John 8:34).

St. Augustine, who more than anyone else shaped the Free-will Defense, nevertheless understood well the human bondage to sin. He took a position between the dualistic Manichaeans, who perceived humans as mere pawns in the battle between Good and Evil, and the optimistic Pelagians, who insisted that humans always had the power to choose the good. In Augustine's view, the first humans had that power in Eden but misused it. As a result, we have inherited an addiction to sin so strong that we are no longer free not to sin. The image of God is now reflected in a cracked mirror: the image has become deformed. In our present "fallen" condition we are "inclined" toward evil, as the Reformation confessions put it.[34]

Inordinate pride and desire, self-seeking and greed, so color all our motives that even our most altruistic actions are tainted. This is not merely a loss of innocence, but an impairment of the pristine freedom to choose without distortion. Humankind has been captivated by lesser goods, the Augustinian argument claims, and what is left of human freedom does not have enough power to set itself straight again. Evil in this view does not arise simply because humans from time to time make bad choices or commit selfish acts; the deeper problem is that evil flows from a distorted heart.

d. *Structures of Evil.* In our discussion of fallen human nature we have been describing a motivation deep within us, a tendency toward sin that works outward from the center of a person's being. Often, however, evil seems to be embodied in impersonal social structures that pressure or even engulf us from outside ourselves. The oppressive power may be an institution, a corporation, or a government. Walter Wink tells of his despair in confronting such entrenched evil during a four-month sabbatical in the *barrios* and *favelas* of Latin America: "The evils we encountered were so monolithic, so massively supported by our own government, in some cases so anchored in a long history of tyranny, that it scarcely seemed that anything could make a difference."[35] It is this kind of structural evil that most concerns the theologians of liberation.

Sometimes the power that holds us in thrall is less a corporate structure than an ideological construct, such as fascism, racism, sexism, consumerism. Less obviously malignant are cultural creations like science, technology, "the American way of life," or religion itself, all of which can become oppressive "isms." It is, of course, easier to perceive someone else's cultural captivity than our own. Given the inescapably social nature of human existence, it is impossible to escape participation in structural evil, but one's participation may be willing or reluctant, contributory or resistant. We speak of these destructive structures as "demonic" because, like the creatures of Response Two, they are powerful, corrupt beings, alien to the human spirit, seeking in insidious ways to take our souls captive from outside. Yet often we conspire with them, making Faustian bargains for survival or for anticipated personal gain.

There is also a troubling ambiguity about these structures themselves. On the one hand, they are constructed by humans out of the God-given possibilities, which is the reason for their inclusion under the category of "Free Choice." Human decisions establish the governments that hold sway over us, human invention fashions our institutions, human imagination creates the ideas that fascinate us. Like the humans who produce them, these structures have the potential for good or ill: they can empower us or overpower us. When the latter happens, we become enslaved to powers of our own making.

Instead of revulsion and resistance, however, the response to these humanly-created powers gone awry is often enthusiastic participation and obedient adulation. Whether a nation or movement or ideology, their followers give over their own power to this larger cause. The phenomenon bears strong resemblance to what the Hebrew prophets called "idolatry" and the New Testament termed "principalities and powers." Reflecting on his Latin American experience, Wink remarks, "For the first time I sensed that I understood what the biblical language of power was all about."[36] When we perceive how the concurrence of many individual choices can coalesce into an almost god-like demonic power, then we see the possibilities of monstrous evil flowing from free choice. Whether that is sufficient to account for the twentieth century's torrent of destruction, or whether a more cosmic evil must be identified, is a matter deferred until chapter 4.

Our survey of the four responses modifying the premise of divine omnipotence is now complete. All of these positions trace the evil in the world to the existence of a power or powers over against God (though perhaps part of God's creation), which impose limits on the divine capacity to determine the outcome of events. In the next chapter we shall examine responses that reject or redefine the other two premises, benevolence and evil.

Chapter 3

"Where Is God?": Holiness Reconsidered

Our search for an answer to the problem of evil led us in the last chapter to reconsider divine omnipotence. Perhaps God is not literally *all*-powerful. Perhaps there are some things God does not control, some things God cannot change. If so, faith's predicament is resolved, for then God is not responsible for everything that happens to us.

Something about this solution is disquieting, however. The security found in a world totally controlled by God dissolves into total vulnerability if there are some things God cannot do. Could such a God be "our refuge and strength"? Isn't a deity of limited power "too small" to be worthy of worship, however slight the limitation might be? Such unsettling questions prompt us to look for some other answer. Perhaps a better resolution can be found by reconsidering one of the other two premises, divine benevolence or the reality of evil.

Responses Rejecting or Redefining Divine Benevolence

We turn first to four responses rejecting or modifying the premise of God's goodness. The first, which I have termed "despotism," is the outright rejection of God's justice. The other three uphold God's justice by employing a "greater good" argument, justifying evil by the higher good it makes possible.

Response Five: Despotism

Evil is either permitted or willed by God because in relation to other beings God is indifferent or unjust or malicious.

Job complains, "I protest [God's] violence, but no one is listening; no one hears my cry for justice" (Job 19:17, TEV). Job wants to challenge God's justice in a court of law. "Should I take [God] to court? Who would make God go?" (Job 9:19, TEV). Then, moving to direct address, Job flings his complaint at the Silence: "Is it right for you to be so cruel? To despise what you yourself have made? And then to smile on the schemes of wicked men?" (Job 9:19, 10:13, TEV). He even accuses God of maliciousness: "Why use me for target practice?" (Job 7:20, TEV).

Twenty-five centuries later, Elie Wiesel echoes Job's complaint:

> "Blessed be the Name of the Eternal!"
> Why, but why should I bless Him?... Because He had had thousands of children burned in His pits? Because He kept six crematories working night and day, on Sundays and feast days? Because in His great might He had created Auschwitz, Birkenau, Buna, and so many factories of death?...
> I was the accuser, God the accused.[1]

Notice that it is God's goodness that Wiesel questions, not God's power. If such bold indictment of God's justice seems unusual or even blasphemous to us, it may be because the Christian Psalter has excluded the Psalms of lament, so significant to Job and Wiesel. Christians are reticent to express anger toward God, and they are the poorer for it. If God's people have a bone to pick, wouldn't God want to hear it from them? Would the patient and caring God portrayed in the New Testament be offended by our expression of hurt?[2]

Such an outburst may also seem more shocking to those who have never been traumatized by suffering. Yet rage against God's unfairness is a perfectly normal response to the initial impact of injury, as when Job cries out, "I am angry and bitter. I have to speak" (Job 7:11, TEV), or when John Quinlan shouts at his mother, "How can you still love God when He's done this to Karen?" That anger may be beamed directly at God, as with Job, or it may be deflected toward others, as with Quinlan.

Often the anger will abate with time, but not always. Several years ago a friend of mine — let's call her Sheila — lost her father to cancer under circumstances punctuated by excessive and pointless distress. Not only did he suffer from intense physical pain during his last days, as the malignancy spread from his colon to his liver and brain, but he had a vision of Satan coming to take him, an idea from which no one could dissuade him. A year after his death, Sheila still refused to receive communion. Her attendance at worship witnessed to her continuing faith; her refusal to commune testified to her unresolved quarrel with God. Wiesel himself, half a century after Auschwitz, is still contending with God in the tradition of the Hasadim. In *A Jew Today* he pleads, "Wait until the last survivor, the last witness, has joined the long procession of silent ghosts whose judgment one day will resound and shake the earth and its Creator. Wait...."[3]

One of Wiesel's theological interpreters has elevated his quarrel with God to a "Theodicy of Protest."[4] With the Holocaust clearly in view, John K. Roth levels a sweeping indictment of theodicies: "Most theodicies have a fatal flaw: they legitimate evil."[5] Even the value of human freedom is insufficient to justify "the slaughter-bench of history" (Hegel). Roth argues that no conceivable "greater good," in this life or the next, could make up for the waste of human life that human freedom permits. "The irretrievable waste of the past robs God of a perfect alibi."[6] But if Roth will not abide any minimizing of evil, neither will he countenance any dilution of divine omnipotence as defined by Mark 10:27: "All things are possible with God." "If God raised Jesus from the dead, he had the might to thwart the Holocaust long before it ended."[7] Having accentuated the premises of Omnipotence and Evil, Roth has only one remaining recourse.

> A protesting theodicy puts God on trial, and in that process the issue of God's wasteful complicity in evil takes center stage.[8]

> Such a wasteful God cannot be totally benevolent. History itself is God's indictment.[9]

This does not lead Roth to turn away from God, however, for humans cannot do battle with evil on their own. Roth's hope is that human protest will induce God once again to act in history, as in the past, to reduce evil's waste and to heal and restore human life. If that is to happen, "God must make his goodness much more decisive than heretofore."[10] "I hope that God gets his act together a little...no, a lot better...and soon."[11]

Roth makes a rousing statement and scores telling points against any attempt to minimize or excuse evil. Personally, however, I would find it difficult to worship a God who has to be goaded into action, and I wonder what human protest could ever be noisy enough to wake up Roth's God, if Auschwitz itself was insufficient to accomplish that.

Response Six: Judgment

Suffering is God's retributive or corrective judgment on our sinful ways.

There is something deep in the human psyche that says that our suffering is the punishment we have coming to us. The verbal link between the English "pain" and the Latin *"poena"* ("punishment") suggests that our pain is the chastisement we deserve. The connection is almost automatic in such parental reprimands as, "If you hadn't left your toys on the stairs, you wouldn't have fallen." This is the hoary notion of *retribution,* and it is still operative today. One reason for its persistence is that deeds have consequences, and they are, to a degree, predictable: "As you sow, so shall you reap." When this is generalized into a universal theological truth, however, it becomes a ready tool for blaming the victim. Interpreting AIDS as divine punishment is but the most recent use of this ancient concept. Blaming the victim in this way is a strategy frequently employed to shield oneself from another's misfortune, for if suffering operates retributively, then good people (like me) need not worry. If one who holds this view becomes afflicted without any evident misbehavior to merit it, the predictable complaint will be, "Why me?"

The fact that the principle of retribution is also found in other cultures is further testimony to its depth in the human psyche. In Buddhism, Jainism, and Hinduism, for instance, transmigration of souls operates according to the law of *karma.* In Buddhism *karma* is the inexorable consequence of one's prior deeds, so that one's behavior in the previous life determines the circumstances of one's present life, including the amount of suffering. In Hinduism *karma* establishes a person's position in the caste system.[12]

In the Hebrew Bible retribution is the most basic explanation of suffering.[13] Recompense is not always individual, however, for the chastisement may fall on one's family, or on succeeding generations, or the whole nation. In the Ten Commandments it is stated, "I the Lord your God am a jealous God, visiting the iniquity of the fathers upon the children to the third and fourth generation of those who hate me...." (Exod. 20:5). The prophets declared that the destruction of Israel and Judah was God's punishment of the whole people for their social sins, in violation of their covenant with God. Indeed, according to the Eden story all humans have been afflicted because of the sins of their first parents. Ezekiel, by contrast, sought to interpret retribution individualistically. Taking issue with the popular proverb, "The fathers have eaten sour grapes, and the children's teeth are set on edge," Ezekiel declared,

> The son shall not suffer for the iniquity of the father, nor the father suffer for the iniquity of the son; the righteousness of the righteous shall be upon himself, and the wickedness of the wicked shall be upon himself. (Ezek. 18:20)

In the post-exilic period the suffering of the nation seemed so disproportionate to Israel's misdeeds that the day of retribution was postponed to the future: a Day of Judgment that is coming, when good and evil people alike will receive their just recompense.

Despite its prominence in Hebrew thinking, retribution had vigorous critics within the Bible. The Psalms of lament indignantly reproach God for the suffering of the righteous and the prosperity of the wicked. Job satirizes the traditional doctrine by placing its precepts on the lips of Job's "comforters." Isaiah enunciates the novel idea that the affliction of God's servant is not punishment for his own misdeeds, but vicarious suffering to bring about healing (Isa. 53:4–5). Isaiah's vision of vicarious suffering is the basis for the concept of redemptive judgment discussed below.

In the New Testament the doctrine of retribution is often assumed, as in the story of the healing of the paralytic in Mark 2:1–12 and the judgment of Ananias and Sapphira in Acts 5:1–11, but the force of the doctrine is undermined, particularly in the teachings of Jesus. "For he makes his sun rise on the evil and on the good, and sends rain on the just and on the unjust," we read in the Sermon on the Mount (Matt. 5:45). Similarly, Jesus refuses to find retribution in Pilate's murder of the Galileans at the altar, or in the death of those on whom the tower of Siloam fell, or in the man born blind (Luke 13:1–5; John 9).[14] In Wolfgang Schrage's opinion, suffering as divine judgment plays less of a role in the New Testament than in subsequent church history.[15]

As a defense of God's goodness, retribution assumes that it is just for sinners to suffer pain and anguish in payment for their misdeeds. Far from compromising God's justice, the tribulations of the wicked balance the scales of justice: "An eye for an eye and a tooth for a tooth." The Hatfields and the Mc-Coys followed this rule, and today many use it to defend capital punishment.

A different theology of divine judgment understands it not as retributive but redemptive. In this view the good to be achieved is not the balancing of the scales of justice ("two wrongs don't make a right"), but the correction and even transformation of the sinner. The Prodigal Son, for instance, found himself in the pigsty as a consequence of his choice of lifestyle. "Fitting reward," some might have said. "You made your bed; now lie in it." Yet the Prodigal's comeuppance was not the point of the story. Life in the pigsty brought him to his senses, creating an opening for grace.

Sometimes human suffering is seen as simultaneously retributive and redemptive. In his second inaugural address Lincoln spoke of the judgment of God, who "gives to both North and South this terrible war, as the woe due to those by whom the offense came." He then spelled out what might be required as recompense for the offense of slavery:

> If God wills that it continue until all the wealth piled by the bondsman's two hundred and fifty years of unrequited toil shall be sunk, and until every drop of blood drawn with the lash shall be paid by another drawn with the sword, as was said three thousand years ago, so still it must be said, "The judgments of the Lord are true and righteous altogether."

Yet in his conclusion, Lincoln made it clear that such harsh retribution was not an end in itself, but was to lead the nation toward healing:

> to bind up the nation's wounds, to care for him who shall have borne the battle and for his widow and his orphan, to do all which may achieve and cherish a just and lasting peace among ourselves and with all nations.[16]

Theologian H. R. Niebuhr similarly discerned the hand of God in World War II, but for him divine judgment was almost wholly redemptive. God's justice, he maintained, is corrective and reconstructive, not vindictive. It seeks to chasten and change the character of sinners rather than merely to punish them for their sins. Furthermore, the redemptive justice of God follows the pattern of Isaiah's suffering servant and the crucified Christ. It is "vicarious in its method, so that the suffering of innocence is used for the remaking of the guilty." "Wars are crucifixions," he affirms, but the cross of vicarious suffering is followed by resurrection. "The response is hopeful in that it regards the time of judgment as also the time of redemption and looks in the midst of tragedy for the emergence of a better order than any which has been realized before."[17]

In summary, "judgment" as an answer to the problem of evil is a "greater good" defense of God's goodness, claiming that the pain and anguish we suffer are necessary either to balance the scales of justice or to bring us to repentance and transformation.

Response Seven: Testing

Affliction is a God-given ordeal to put our faith to the test.
Earlier I presented the story of Dolores, who explained the sequence of illnesses in her life as a divine test. She was familiar with the notion that suffering was God's judgment; indeed, she once told me she interpreted her sister Joan's suffering as divine retribution for Joan's declaration, "There is no God." Apparently she found no fault in herself to account for her own tribulation, however; hence she ascribed her ordeal to the fact that "God is testing us." She even warned her son, who wanted to become a priest, "Maybe God's going to test you, too."

Suffering as a test of one's faith is a frequent biblical theme. "Gold and silver are tested by fire, and a person's heart is tested

by the Lord," we read in Proverbs (17:3),[18] and this is echoed in
the First Letter of Peter: "Even gold, which can be destroyed, is
tested by fire; and so your faith, which is much more precious
than gold, must also be tested, so that it may endure" (1:7, TEV).
The belief is that through tribulation, God is putting faith to the
test, trying its mettle, examining its steadfastness. In this view
suffering is faith's "pop quiz." We should not be misled by the
crucible metaphor. "The salient point of this figure is the testing
and proving, not refining and purifying," Schrage insists. "'In
the fire' of suffering it is revealed what is faith and what is not."[19]

The classic biblical text is the testing of Job. When God brags
to the satan about Job's faithfulness and uprightness, the satan
insinuates doubt: "Would Job worship you if he got nothing out
of it?...But now suppose you take away everything he has —
he will curse you to your face!" (Job 1:9, 11, TEV). God accepts
the dare and allows the satan to put Job to his dreadful test.

In the New Testament Jesus himself is tested before commencing his ministry. In the Lord's Prayer, however, Jesus permits his disciples to ask God to spare them from the trial: "And
do not bring us to the test" (Matt. 6:13, NEB). Paul reiterates
the doctrine of testing, but for him affliction tests not only faith
but also the love that "suffers all things."[20] It is the believer's
duty to endure the test steadfastly, but Paul also promises that
"God...will not allow you to be tested beyond your power to
remain firm." Furthermore, God "will give you strength to endure" (1 Cor. 10:13, TEV). Thus Paul holds that perseverance in
the face of trials is simultaneously a human responsibility and
a divine gift.

According to this response, then, the "greater good" that suffering serves is tried and true faith, effective in love.

Response Eight: Personal Growth

*To achieve maturity, persons need to overcome hardship, anguish,
and defeat.*

According to this perspective, initially sketched in chapter 1,
the divine purpose in creating humans is "soul-making": to
bring into being a community of mature persons for fellowship
with God and with one another. By definition, maturity is that
stage in an organism's life at which it reaches the goal of its
development. In humans, maturity signifies both a stage of life

and a quality of character attainable only through a lengthy process of facing crises, overcoming obstacles, and taking risks. Although "mature" is a relative term (as in "mature for her years") and cannot be correlated with a specific age, no one is born mature. Even omnipotence could not create beings mature at birth, for "born mature" is a contradiction in terms, as nonsensical as "married bachelors." Maturation is a process not to be shortcut. Like a good parent, God must patiently await the step-by-step development of character, eschewing intervention even when bad decisions are made. This process inevitably results in a lot of pain and suffering, some of which is essential to the process itself, and some of which is its inevitable by-product.

Because maturation is a natural process, this response could be considered a form of "Natural Order." It also resembles "Free Choice" in requiring human freedom and responsibility, but instead of freedom itself being the higher good that justifies the permission of evil, the greater good is the development of mature selves, together with the fellowship that this makes possible.

This position has roots in the biblical view of suffering as God's *paideia,* divine pedagogy. In most biblical texts expressing this view, the instrument of instruction is the rod of God; hence it is difficult to distinguish between divine pedagogy and redemptive judgment. "Blessed is the man whom thou dost chasten, O Lord, and whom thou dost teach out of thy law," says the psalmist (Ps. 93:12). That thought is echoed in Hebrews: "For the moment all discipline seems painful rather than pleasant; later it yields the peaceful fruit of righteousness to those who have been trained by it" (Heb. 12:11). In Romans 5, Paul views suffering as educational without implying punishment, stating that "suffering produces endurance, and endurance produces character, and character produces hope" (Rom. 5:3–4).[21]

In recent years John Hick has constructed a full-blown theodicy giving powerful expression to this interpretation of human suffering. In fact, the publication in 1966 of his *Evil and the God of Love* seems to have precipitated the present flood of volumes on suffering and evil.[22] Taking Keats's "Vale of Soul-making" as his motto, Hick sets out to produce a contemporary "Irenaean Theodicy" that follows the thinking of second-century Bishop Irenaeus instead of echoing the dominant Western theodicy derived from Augustine's doctrine of the Fall.

Hick begins by presenting the unvarnished facts of evil that need to be reconciled with "the limitless power and goodness of God":[23]

Can a world in which sadistic cruelty often has its way, in which selfish lovelessness is so rife, in which there are debilitating diseases, crippling accidents, bodily and mental decay, insanity, and all manner of natural disasters be regarded as the expression of infinite creative goodness?[24]

Hick approaches this task teleologically, interpreting suffering and evil as instrumental to an anticipated perfection in the future rather than as the result of a fall from perfection in the past. God's purpose in creating humans, he claims, is to bring into being finite persons who, through their own free actions, will come to know and love their maker and embrace the value of mutual, self-giving love. A crucial step in Hick's argument is his claim that "virtues which have been formed within the agent as a hard won deposit of his own right decisions in situations of challenge and temptation, are intrinsically more valuable than virtues created within him ready made and without any effort on his own part."[25] These "intrinsically more valuable virtues" constitute the greater good that justifies the existence of evil in the world.

Hick gives three reasons why evil is unavoidable if these more valuable virtues are to emerge. First, humans who begin life free but immature will inevitably fall into error and sin in the process of actualizing that freedom and growing toward maturity. Second, the human environment must be dangerous, including both moral and natural evil, so that persons can develop the desired virtues by accepting challenges, confronting hardships, and coping with failure, misery, and defeat. Third, in order that humans may come to love God freely rather than being overawed by the divine love, they must be placed in an ambiguous world that could be perceived either as God's creation or as a purely natural system; yet that distancing from God makes it possible for humans to turn away from God in sin, as well as turn toward God in faith. "There could not be a person-making world devoid of what we call evil," Hick concludes, "and evils are never tolerable — except for the sake of greater goods which may come out of them."[26]

Hick anticipates two objections. First, he admits that the greatest challenge to the plausibility of his theodicy is "the sheer amount and intensity of both moral and natural evil."[27] To some, the cost will appear to outweigh the gain, especially those in the throes of horrendous suffering. Yet he insists that "if we take with full seriousness the value of human freedom and responsibility, as essential to the eventual creation of perfected children of God, then we cannot consistently want God to revoke that freedom when its wrong exercise becomes intolerable to us." The ultimate outcome "is worth any finite suffering in the course of its creation."[28]

The second anticipated objection is that in this lifetime most people never reach the full maturity Hick has in mind. He quotes Erich Fromm: "The tragedy in the life of most of us is that we die before we are fully born."[29] Hence there must be some arena of existence beyond this earthly life where the process of person-making will come to completion. "Without such an eschatological fulfillment, this theodicy would collapse," he concedes.[30]

Hick's theodicy has elicited much criticism, as one might expect in response to such a *tour de force*. Many of these objections can be embraced in the generalization that it explains both too much and too little. It explains too much by justifying and thereby minimizing the very evils that Hick deplores. It explains too little because so many of the world's ills serve no educational purpose, often breaking their victims instead of building character.

•

Looking back over these last three responses — judgment, testing, growth — we find that all three seek to defend God's goodness by showing that the evils we endure are necessary to produce a greater good. They therefore succeed only to the extent that the evils permitted do, indeed, contribute to a higher good achievable in no other way. The trouble is, the punishment usually doesn't fit the crime, the test often overwhelms the victim, and too many souls are lost in the vale of soul-making. There is truth in these responses, but the world's suffering is altogether too excessive and too inappropriate to these goals to be fully explained by them.

A further objection to these and any greater good argument is that they tend to minimize the evilness of evil, if not explain it away altogether. If an apparent evil contributes to a greater good, should we continue to regard it as evil at all? Are we not in the position of the members of Pascack Bible Church, for whom the premature deaths of five teenagers are of no ultimate importance, because they are not worth comparing to the greater value of God's plan? To the extent that the positions we have been considering succeed in denying that the evils we deplore are actually evil at all, these responses really belong in the next category, the denial of evil.

Responses Denying or Redefining Evil

Response Nine: Illusion

The ills we seem to suffer are actually illusory, the result of erroneous thinking.

"There is nothing either good or bad, but thinking makes it so," Rosencrantz assures Guildenstern.[31] William James seems to agree:

> Much of what we call evil is due entirely to the way men take the phenomenon.... Since you make [the facts] evil or good by your own thoughts about them, it is the ruling of your thoughts which proves to be your principal concern.[32]

Clearly the way we think about an unpleasant event can magnify it into a tragic evil, reduce it to a mere nuisance, or transform it into a positive challenge. We all know persons who amplify or even fabricate the ills they suffer by their attitude toward them. When this common observation is elevated to a complete explanation for evil, then we have the response labeled *illusion.* The Hindu philosopher Shankara taught that the world of experience is a dream world (*maya*), and that believing in its reality and value is what gives rise to the endless cycle of human suffering.[33] In Buddhism the source of suffering (*dukka*) is the illusory belief in a self. "We conjure up such ideas as 'I' and 'mine,' and many most undesirable states result." The paradoxical truth is that only when we get rid of self can we be really happy.[34]

The classic example of this response among Western religions is Christian Science. Believing that Divine Spirit is wholly good and all-inclusive ("all-in-all"), Christian Science holds that the afflictions humans think they suffer, including death, are actually misperceptions of reality. They are the result of misunderstanding, the consequence of faulty belief. Evil is a lie. It is not real at all. It is literally nothing.

Christian Science solves the problem of evil by discarding the assumption of evil altogether. Yet even so drastic a move does not entirely dispose of evil, transposing it instead into the mental realm. If our affliction is due to erroneous belief, then that flawed thinking is itself the evil that must be addressed, for those erroneous ideas still diminish, destroy, and oppress us. Mary Baker Eddy tacitly recognizes this in speaking of "the awful unreality called evil."[35] The "*un*-reality" is still "awful."

Response Ten: Partial Perspective

Although the evils we experience are real, if they could be viewed from a more inclusive perspective, they would be seen to contribute to a larger, harmonious whole.

The discernment of good or evil always depends on a person's perspective: there is at least this much validity in the position staked out by "illusion." The old proverb says that one person's meat is another's poison. In Lancaster County, Pennsylvania, renowned for both its agriculture and its tourism, a day of rain will bring gratitude from the farmers, but grumbling from the tourists. A more shocking illustration is provided by the colonizers of New England. During the three years prior to the arrival of the Pilgrims in 1620, the native American population was decimated by a deadly epidemic (probably smallpox, contracted from an English slave trader). One Puritan divine, noting that mortality was heaviest among "young men and children, the very seeds of increase," celebrated the natives' calamity as "The Wonderful Preparation the Lord Christ by His Providence Wrought for His People's Abode in this Western World."[36]

Perhaps the perception of evil is always a function of one's limited angle of vision. Perhaps if we could see things from God's eye view, it would all look different.

> For my thoughts are not your thoughts,
> Neither are your ways my ways,
> says the Lord.
> For as the heavens are higher than the earth,
> so are my ways higher than your ways
> and my thoughts than your thoughts. (Isa. 55:8–9)

Alexander Pope has given *partial perspective* its classic formulation.

> All nature is but art, unknown to thee;
> All chance, direction, which thou canst not see;
> All discord, harmony not understood;
> All partial evil, universal good;
> And spite of pride, in erring reason's spite,
> One truth is clear, whatever is, is right.[37]

The controlling metaphors in this passage are the contrasting images of harmony and discord, of part and whole. The "thou" being addressed is humankind, one species within the entire chain of being. The human mistake is to judge the whole from the myopic viewpoint of one part. Instead of accepting its proper place within the comprehensive good of the whole, humankind pridefully judges things from its own partial perspective. Pride in turn leads reason into error in criticizing the way things are. If we were able to adopt God's view of the whole, then we would understand that what sounds like discord is really harmony, what looks like evil from a partial viewpoint is actually good for the whole, and "whatever is, is right."

One cannot, of course, take God's viewpoint of the whole, but what makes this response credible is the common experience of changing one's mind when looking back on a traumatic event. A case in point is Catherine Marshall's account of her husband's sudden death in midlife, at the peak of his career. Sometime after his funeral, she began to question God's will in the matter.

> "Why, God, why did it have to end this way?" I asked over and over. We had sure evidence that Christ was with us that night when the final heart attack struck. But if that was true, why did He not stretch out His hand and cure Peter's damaged heart? We had believed in healing. We

had seen it, witnessed it in our family. Why, then, was he not healed?[38]

In a short time something happened to change her perspective.

> Within a matter of weeks, the way opened for the pub-
> lication of a book of Peter's sermons. That book was
> to become a best seller. Through its pages, Peter would
> preach to thousands of people, whom he could never have
> reached, were he still with us in the flesh.[39]

Her initial doubts disappeared once she saw things from a larger vantage point. *Partial perspective* does not nullify the evil for everyone, however. Rabbi Kushner, whose book, like Marshall's, enabled him to reach a larger audience, refused to accept his increased effectiveness as justification for his son's death: "I would give up all of those gains in a second if I could have my son back."[40]

Atheism and Agnosticism

The ten responses considered so far complete the list of responses that attempt to offer a justification for the Creator's permission of evil. The remaining two positions refuse to accept any such reasons (or combination thereof) as sufficient justification for the existence of evil. The first of these regards the reality of evil as a conclusive argument against the existence of God; the second pleads agnosticism (literally, "not knowing") due to the limitations of human knowledge and falls back on mystery.

Response Eleven: Atheism

The reality of evil in the world makes belief in God impossible.
This position simply follows the three premises through to their logical conclusion. If the evil in the world must be regarded as genuine, and God is, by definition, both omnipotent and perfectly good in the strongest sense of those terms, then it is logically impossible that such a being exists, for the very definition of deity is contradicted by the reality of evil. "Why do I suffer? That is the rock of atheism," claims Georg Büchner.[41]

We have already seen that many persons, some of them once believers, find themselves driven to this conclusion in the face of undeniable evil.

Response Twelve: Mystery

A problem such as this, involving the power and purpose of the infinite God, is beyond the capacity of finite minds to solve.

After examining the previous eleven responses, some readers will doubtless be ready to select "none of the above." Even if one agrees with much of what has been asserted in these responses, there always seems to be a remainder of ugly facts that can neither be explained nor excused. And if allowance is made for that by acknowledging the limitations of our partial perspective, then evil becomes trivialized: what was first encountered as horrendous has become justified as contributing to some larger good. The believer is inclined to conclude from all this that we are up against a mystery too deep for human minds to fathom. Alan Paton acknowledged just that: "There is a wound in the Creation, and it groans and travails until now, and I don't know why."[42]

We might have anticipated such a conclusion, for if macrocosmic and microcosmic events in the universe defy human comprehension, why should we expect to understand the ways of the One who is said to transcend the world infinitely? "There are more things in heaven and earth, Horatio, than are dreamt of in your philosophy."[43] Religion springs from awe before the unfathomable Holy, and so faith has always spoken of divine mystery. Religion does not just flee to mystery after reasons fail; faith *begins* in mystery before groping to give that awesome experience meaning through metaphors and myths. Isn't it enough, then, to live in the confidence of God's love without requiring explanations? Why try to unscrew the inscrutable? Wasn't Father Donnelly's first answer the best one: "There are no answers — none at all"?

Here the skeptic will rightly object that the believer is "copping out." How is it, the skeptic asks, that believers claim confidently to *know* God loves them, yet appeal to God's *unknowability* when asked about the divine permission of evil? It is precisely the reality of evil in the world that most counts against that divine love in which the believer so confidently trusts. Furthermore, it is unethical to believe in anything without sufficient reason; such a stance is scarcely distinguishable from superstition.

Believers are trapped in a dilemma. If they seek an explanation for the apparent incompatibility of God and evil, then it seems that they are trying to take heaven by storm. Yet if they rest their case in mystery, they run the risk of naive credulity, or even of believing self-contradictory nonsense. There really is no escape from this predicament, so we must be content with trying to "muddle through," as the British so aptly put it. There are no final answers, but surely some answers are better than others. So we seek the best answers we can find, all the while acknowledging the circumambient mystery.

A Personal Conclusion

Now that the smorgasbord of possible solutions to the problem of evil has been sampled, the reader has a right to ask which responses the author himself selects. Certainly any approach to the riddle of evil begins and ends in *mystery*. Awe in the face of mystery is our proper stance before the finite universe, its infinite source and intricate pattern, and the enigmatic evil that infiltrates the world and implicates its maker. And when our reasonings come to an end, we shall still have to confess that there is much that is beyond human comprehension. "The professor would like to understand what is not understandable," remarked a physician-survivor of the death camps to Robert Jay Lifton during his investigation into Nazi genocide. "We ourselves who were there, and who have always asked ourselves the question and will ask it until the end of our lives, we will never understand it, because it cannot be understood."[44]

More specifically for myself, there are unanswered questions concerning both natural and moral evil. I do not, for instance, understand why there should be a place for cancer in God's good creation, or why the human cycle of life and death needs to terminate in the tortuous and undignified way that it so often does. Nor can I see why human freedom should be so susceptible to destructive attitudes and behaviors such as Nazism, or why God's redeeming work has not proved more effective in curing such behaviors. I admit that my inability to understand may be due to myopic vision, so to "mystery" I add *partial perspective,* although I refuse to accept that position as a comprehensive explanation of all the evils one might encounter. *Illusion* also plays some role, for perhaps more than I would like to believe, my horror arises from fearful unwillingness to accept my own finitude.

Indeed, there is doubtless some truth in each response. Consider *testing,* for instance. Although I find it impossible to believe that the gracious God revealed in Jesus Christ selects persons for affliction as a test or trial, I recognize that the crucible of suffering can temper faith, and that crises can lead persons to re-examine the direction of their lives. Similarly concerning *judgment,* I totally reject the notion that God sends suffering as punishment, yet there is undeniable truth in the causal relationship between behaviors and consequences. Clogged arteries are the price we pay for fatty foods, lung cancer is the risk we run in smoking, children of alcoholics are more likely to become alcoholics, and so on. Such examples, however, come closer to illustrating the regularities of natural order than manifesting divine judgment.

The responses that are central to my own understanding of suffering and evil are *natural order* and *free choice,* which must be seen as interrelated. These two positions, I am convinced, are so much a part of the air we breathe today that they are quite inescapable. All of us conduct our daily lives assuming that we can count on the principle of cause and effect and the regularities of the physical world. Would anyone prefer an undependable world, even if we could be sure that God would always intervene to make things turn out right? And yet we know that we are sometimes badly hurt by those very regularities on which we have come to rely.

We count on a similar consistency in interpersonal relations. Every day, agreements are made and obligations assumed. We take it for granted that those promises have been made freely, and that it is reasonable to hold persons accountable for their actions. We sometimes get burned by that assumption also! Yet would anyone really prefer a world in which some power would always override us whenever we make a bad choice or fail to follow through on our commitments? Do we not prize the responsibility and freedom that go with being human too much to wish for such a world? We really cannot have it both ways. It is impossible — logically impossible — to have an ordered world populated by genuinely free beings in which God would intervene every time something threatened to go wrong. The ordered universe would quickly dissolve into a world in which God alone called every shot. My conviction, based on our common human experience as well as scripture, is that we do inhabit an ordered world of responsibility, and that God faithfully respects that structure and freedom, even when its evil consequences bring pain to God and injury to God's children.

Closely linked to free choice, and presupposing it, is *personal growth.* I agree with Hick's judgment regarding a pain-free environment: "A world in which there can be no pain or suffering would also be one in which there can be no moral choices and hence no possibility of moral growth and development."[45] Simone Weil puts it more succinctly: "If there were no affliction we should be able to believe ourselves in Paradise. Horrid possibility."[46] A world in which free persons confront the challenges of hardship, adversity, and loss is essential to the development of those values we most prize as the mark of true humanity. Yet the limited but genuine truth in this response becomes repugnant when it is extended to cover the entire range of human suffering. Here Hick, it seems to me, is hoisted on his own petard: "It is this almost inevitable pretension of theodicy to a cosmic vantage point that provokes the thought that any solution to the problem of evil must be worse than the problem itself!"[47]

Returning to *free choice,* I must lift up another element in that response, for it seems that the evil in the world today far exceeds that which can be accounted for by natural disasters, bad choices, and personal growth. Greed, exploitation, violence, and oppression have run rampant in our time in a way that staggers the imagination, especially when we humans try to think of ourselves as rational, well-meaning creatures. How does one explain that we are hell-bent on suicide through a nuclear arms race, through pollution of the atmosphere, through stripping the topsoil on which our food supply depends? How does one account for our tendency toward destruction, including self-destruction? Freud postulated a "death-instinct" and Fromm talked about "necrophilia" (love of death). The Reformers, drawing on the tradition of the Fall, said simply, "By nature I am prone to hate God and my neighbor."[48] Somehow God's reflection in us has become grossly distorted. I resist such notions, especially when applied to myself and those I love, and yet, how do we explain our human behavior other than through some such destructive tendency that has vitiated the image of God in us?

But perhaps that's laying too heavy a burden on the human species, to the point of blaming the victim. Should we humans really accept responsibility for all the evil in the world? Furthermore, even the notion of individual perversity seems inadequate to account for the enormous social evils of our era. As we read the signs of the times, does it not appear that we are more the victims of malignant forces beyond our control than the culprits who cause them? "Evil seems almost bigger than something that human beings can bring about by themselves," concludes Daniel Simundson after examining the story of the Fall.[49] Are we then driven toward some superhuman source of evil, a cosmic demonic power? Does some form of the first or second responses come closer to the reality of evil? Or is the human potential for evil really sufficient to account for it? That is the issue we must address in our next chapter.

Chapter 4

"The Devil Made Me Do It": Demonic Power and Human Responsibility

"There's a force, a dark, flowing force, that goes right through our minds, right through our minds and bodies, that carries us toward evil." That opening line from the television special "Facing Evil with Bill Moyers" poses the issue to be addressed in this chapter. The speaker of those words, ethicist and self-styled skeptic Philip Hallie, harbors no doubt concerning the reality of that force. "I see it in so many ways, that there is such a force."[1] His statement leaves open the question whether this dark force that "carries us toward evil" arises from within human nature, or whether it invades our being from beyond.

Yet paradoxically, even as we approach the end of this violent century, people seem reluctant to speak of evil. "Few grown-ups want to come right out and say the E word," asserts *Newsweek* in its review of a children's exhibit on the Holocaust.[2] That is confirmed by an informal poll I have been conducting among church people, fully a third of whom say it is not a word they use. To understand this paradox, we need to look at both the popular connotations of the term and our changing cultural perspectives toward evil. Before exploring the substance of Hallie's statement, therefore, we will sharpen our definition of evil and trace the changing perceptions of its reality in this century.

Defining Evil

We have already observed that "evil" is an antonym for "good" and that each of the two terms is defined by its contrast with the other. There is, however, another antonym for "good," namely, "bad," and people have no similar reluctance to use this word.

It should prove instructive, then, to examine the differences in the way we use these two words.

"Dad, that's a bad joke." My son says that often, and there's no puzzle about what he means: it's an assessment of the quality of my humor. But suppose he were to say instead, "Dad, that's an *evil* joke." I would first of all be startled by the intensity of that criticism. "Evil" is an expression of extreme censure, usually reserved for moments of outrage, as when a horrified witness to a cruel deed shouts, "That's an *evil* thing to do!"

I would also wonder exactly what he was criticizing in labeling my joke "evil," for "evil" is not a term used to evaluate quality of humor. Perhaps my witticism was disparaging to someone present — an ethnic slur or sexist remark — causing injury to that person. In that case, it was an evil joke because it resulted in an evil consequence. More likely, he would be criticizing my motive in telling it, whether it actually hurt anyone or not. When we call an act "evil," we almost always mean that the perpetrator maliciously intended harm. The fact that "evil" could refer either to the consequence of my joke or to my motive in telling it highlights the twofold use we make of this term: there are evils that persons *intend,* which we commonly classify as moral evil or sin, and there are evils that persons *undergo,* such as all the types of suffering we listed in chapter 1. The two often go together, but not always. Malicious intent may be thwarted, but it remains evil nonetheless; tornadoes are not "intended" by anyone, but they still result in evil consequences. So there are two kinds of evil: evil intent (moral evil or sin) and evil undergone (suffering), and neither can be subsumed under the definition of the other.[3] In ordinary speech, we most often use "evil" to refer to intent — to wickedness or malevolence.

Two differences in our common use of "evil" and "bad" have now surfaced. First, "evil" is a much stronger term of disapproval, implying extreme censure, and second, it is usually a judgment of motive or intent. These nuances alone might lead us to use "evil" sparingly.

A third difference is that "evil" is often used as a noun referring to negative power or powers. Hallie speaks of evil as "a dark, flowing force," and M. Scott Peck defines it as "that force, residing either inside or outside of human beings, that seeks to kill life or liveliness."[4] There is no equivalent use of "bad." Whether or not evil exists is an important philosophical question, but it would be grammatically odd to ask, "Does bad exist?"

This substantive use points to another reason why talk of evil is rare. Walter Wink asserts that "our culture resolutely refuses to believe in the real existence of evil." He claims that people would rather regard it as "a kind of systems breakdown that can be fixed with enough tinkering."[5] I recall a college professor who preferred to speak of "the maladjustment of an organism to its environment." Many of the church people in my poll said they were more comfortable describing persons as "sick" rather than "evil." The resistance becomes even greater if there is any suggestion that evil is a supernatural power. By the beginning of the twentieth century, Satan had quietly disappeared from the scene, states William Tremmel in his history of Satan. "No one said it blatantly, but from Goethe to Shaw the quiet conclusion had been drawn: Satan does not really exist."[6] Wink suggests, "If you want to bring all talk to a halt in shocked embarrassment, every eye riveted on you, try mentioning angels, or demons, or the devil."[7]

What makes such talk of evil, especially occult evil, so difficult for us is that we are heirs of the Enlightenment. We belong to the era of scientific and historical thinking, which interprets the forces shaping our lives as natural and human. From this point of view, deeply ingrained in all of us educated in this century, whatever people mean by "evil" can better be described in terms drawn from the natural and behavioral sciences, so we try to make evil fit within that framework of interpretation. Along with scientific-historical thinking goes trust in technology and confidence in progress. Two centuries ago Condorcet enunciated the hope of human perfectibility, optimistically predicting that once bad laws and institutions had been reformed and ignorance and prejudice banished, men and women would be free and warfare would cease.[8] That optimism was still strong at the beginning of this century, and even at mid-century many still held the belief voiced by Anne Frank less than a month before her arrest: "In spite of everything I still believe that people are really good at heart."[9] If that is the case, then whatever may be wrong with humankind can be remedied by education or therapy or through reforming our institutions.

To be sure, that optimistic worldview had already received a severe blow early in this century. Warfare, instead of disappearing from human history, took on a fury hitherto unknown. On July 1, 1916, what was thought to be impossible in this civilized century, happened. On a single day at the Battle of the Somme, twenty thousand British soldiers were slaughtered — one-third the number of Americans killed in the entire Vietnam conflict. Another million fell in the ensuing five months, fighting over less than one hundred square miles of land.[10] Yet the old optimism lived on in the reassurance that this was "the war to end all wars."

Within a generation there ensued another world conflagration, with even greater devastation, displacement, and loss of life. Once again the impossible happened: Auschwitz — so incredible that those who discovered it could not believe their eyes, and some refuse to believe it yet. Six million Jews were exterminated by the most educated and cultured people in the history of civilization. Since then the *Holocaust* has become the paradigmatic symbol for evil, the test case for every theodicy.[11] In the eighteenth century it was the 1755 Lisbon earthquake with its 100,000 victims that epitomized evil and tested regnant theologies, but in the twentieth century it is human disasters that perplex us most — the Battle of the Somme, the "killing fields" of Cambodia, famine in Ethiopia, and above all, the Holocaust.

Yet even these awful events did not completely dispel the dream of progress. Worldviews change slowly. Exactly at mid-century I entered Yale Divinity School in a class largely populated by war veterans, some scarred by memories too painful to talk about. Yet we were an idealistic class, certain that we would not pass on to our children the same "snafued" world we had inherited from our parents. To be sure, our professors intoned the phrase "two world wars and a depression" as a ritual incantation intended to remind us of human depravity and point us to the redemption found only through God's grace. We repeated that phrase often enough, but we only half accepted the sobering realism it was intended to convey. After all, that generation of ex-G.I.'s had not just won a victory; they had totally demolished the great fascist dictatorships. The slogan of the Seabees still echoed in our heads: "The difficult we do immediately; the impossible takes a little longer."

The idealism of my generation peaked in the sixties and then disintegrated in disillusionment. Today war, terrorism, torture, genocide are daily fare, not to mention drugs and AIDS. Even schoolchildren are aware of the ease with which "Nuclear Winter" could become a reality — and that is but one of numerous possible ways in which the human species could commit "omnicide."[12] Meanwhile, experts warn us that our economy is rusting, the U.S. is in decline, and that today's college graduates must expect a lower standard of living than that of their parents.

Many now look to the approaching twenty-first century not with the enthusiastic anticipation of a decade or two ago, but with dark apprehension. Not only are we passing on to our children a botched-up world, but one that may not be around very long for them to enjoy. The times have an apocalyptic feel, as if we were about to participate in some great cataclysm. The apocalyptic mood is especially evident in the spate of disaster movies that began a dozen years ago with *Poseidon Adventure* and *Towering Inferno.* Many films from this period also break the "good guys vs. bad guys" formula, portraying instead a deeply defiled world in which evil is pervasive. In *Chinatown,* the protagonist finds himself entangled in a constantly-expanding web of corruption until, threatened from every side, he no longer knows if there is anyone in the world whom he can trust.

Once people become accustomed to thinking this way, the question naturally arises whether the source and power of evil do not transcend human existence. It is no surprise, therefore, that belief in occult powers is on the rise. In 1964, polls showed that 37 percent of the population believed in Satan's existence, but that was up to 50 percent by 1973 (about the time *The Exorcist* was playing), and it has continued to rise.[13]

So Hallie's conviction that there is "a dark, flowing force, that goes right through our minds" is much in tune with the mood of the times. That view is by no means unanimous, however. On the same program with Hallie, Barbara Jordan, herself no stranger to evil, stated a somewhat different opinion:

> I do not feel that evil is some outside force separated from the individual. I believe that in human nature, in each individual, there is a bad and a good, or an evil and a good.[14]

Unfortunately, there was no discussion of the differences between Hallie's and Jordan's positions. The question that needed to be addressed to Jordan's viewpoint is one posed by Wink in another context: "The sheer massiveness of evil in the world point[s] to a more malevolent source than the isolated infidelities of puny human beings."[15] The issue then is this: can human choices alone account for the social evil of our time, or does its sheer massiveness point to a power that transcends human control and holds us in its grip?

Social Evil and Social Research

Along with this new sense of the reality and depth of evil, then, there is an urgent need to re-examine what the power of evil actually is, how it arises, and why it has secured such a tenacious grip on the human spirit in our century. Such an investigation is, in fact, already well underway, as any survey of recent books on evil will show. Because in this century the question is posed by large-scale social evil, only an interpretation of social evil's exponential power will provide a satisfactory answer. Hence it is not surprising that social scientists have been in the forefront of contemporary inquiries into evil. From the extensive social research already undertaken, we will examine three published studies of social evil that seem to hold special promise for theological reflection: Stanley Milgram's obedience experiments, M. Scott Peck's study of the My Lai massacre, and Robert Jay Lifton's research on Nazi doctors.

In a now-famous set of experiments on obedience, Yale psychologist Stanley Milgram demonstrated that ordinary people will administer pain to innocent victims if ordered to do so by authority.[16] Between 1960 and 1963, Milgram recruited over a thousand volunteers, a cross-section of the local populace, to participate in his experiment. The volunteers were told that they would be subjects in an experiment to measure the effects of punishment on learning. The experiment itself began with the subject watching as a "learner" (really an actor) was strapped into a chair and his wrists connected to electrodes. Then the subject was taken by the experimenter to an adjacent room and seated before an imposing shock-generator, capable of delivering to the "learner" a shock ranging from 15 to 450 volts. At the upper end of the scale a warning was printed on the machine: "DANGER — SEVERE SHOCK." The subject was instructed to deliver a shock to the "learner" each time a wrong answer was given, beginning at the bottom of the scale and increasing the dosage by fifteen volts each time. The "learner" (who, unbeknown to the subject, was actually receiving no shock) responded audibly to the shocks, from a groan at the 75-volt level to an agonized scream at 285 volts. Whenever the subject demurred, the white-coated experimenter ordered the subject to continue, although the experimenter had no power to compel the subject to go on.

To Milgram's surprise and dismay, 65 percent of the volunteers continued all the way to the 450-volt level, even though they had nothing personally to gain from doing so. The experiment has been repeated at other universities, in other cultures, and with both sexes, always with the same results. Milgram concludes,

> Ordinary people, simply doing their jobs, and without any particular hostility on their part, can become agents in a terrible destructive process. Moreover, even when the destructive effects of their work become patently clear, and they are asked to carry out actions incompatible with fundamental standards of morality, relatively few people have the resources needed to resist authority.[17]

Milgram's conclusions are significant for any consideration of human evil and anticipate the findings of subsequent research. Ordinary people — two out of three drawn from a cross-section of society — will obey commands that conflict with their own moral principles if ordered to do so by someone vested with authority. This was true even in the absence of any sanctions to enforce obedience: Milgram's subjects were free to walk away at any time, without penalty. If this is the case where authority operates without disciplinary sanctions, how much greater will be the inclination to obey an evil command in a situation where authority is backed by power to reward and punish. Few people, Milgram concludes, have the moral strength to resist commands that they perceive to be immoral. Later in this chapter Peck describes a battlefield situation and Lifton a death-camp environment in which there was an "extreme lack of restraint." If ordinary persons cannot resist immoral commands in the civilized atmosphere of a university, how will they resist in barbaric situations characterized by extreme lack of restraint?

In Milgram's post-experiment interviews, subjects typically excused their actions by saying, "I wouldn't have done it by myself. I was just doing what I was told" — an explanation, Milgram observes, that is reminiscent of Nuremberg. One should not conclude, however, that the experimental subjects lacked conscience. Milgram explains that during the course of the experiment, the ethical concerns of the subjects shift away from their own moral standards "to a consideration of how well [they are] living up to the expectations that the authority has." This is the moral equivalent of "When in Rome, do as the Romans." After the experiment, subjects revert to their previous moral sensitivities, as evidenced by their need to justify their actions. This shifting back and forth between two incompatible sets of moral expectations is the basis for the concept of "doubling," developed by Lifton to explain how Nazi doctors were able to perform deeds that contradicted their personal standards and medical ideals (see below pp. 76–78).

Most subjects further justified their actions during the interview by invoking a noble cause, usually the advancement of scientific knowledge. In a scientifically-oriented culture like ours, such a justification was undoubtedly invited by the use of white coats and impressive-looking equipment. This appeal to a culturally-valued cause is a tiny prefiguration of the role of ideology in providing a motive for evil, as reported by all our other researchers.

Still another justification recurring in the interviews was, "He was so stupid and stubborn he deserved to get shocked." That statement excuses cruelty by employing the twin strategies of devaluing and blaming the victim. Both strategies, augmented in force, will reappear in subsequent research as "enemy creation" and "scapegoating."

An important dynamic built into the experiment was its incremental structure, which moved the subjects into increasing brutality one small step at a time. Psychologist David G. Myers comments on the importance of this phenomenon for understanding evil:

> This subtle step-by-step entrapment is one of the most heinous dynamics of evil. The Nazis steadily escalated the cruelty their people inflicted on the Jews, and in similar fashion the Vietnam War was inexorably escalated.[18]

Milgram notes that the momentum toward evil is also furthered by the tendency of an agency or institution — in this case the experiment — to assume its own impersonal authority. Often the experimenter could overcome resistance simply by stating, "The experiment *requires* that you continue," an imperative that sounds more authoritative than a mere individual's command. This illustrates the way in which a humanly-created movement or institution acquires its own momentum and authority, transcending that of its participants.

Milgram developed a number of variations on his basic experiment. In one of these, the subject was put in the same room with the "learner," close enough to touch. This significantly increased resistance to continuing the experiment, demonstrating the importance of "distancing" between perpetrator and victim. Even so, almost one-third were still willing to go all the way to the end. In another variation, the subject was not the one to deliver the shocks, but participated by administering the word-pair test to the "learner." Under these circumstances, ninety-two percent were willing to carry the experiment to its conclusion. Milgram notes that "it is psychologically easy to ignore responsibility when one is only an intermediate link in a chain of evil action." He suggests that perhaps such fragmentation of responsibility "is the most common character of organized evil in modern society."[19]

Many of the social dynamics uncovered in Milgram's research were repeated in two other famous experiments: Ronald Jones's "Third Wave" simulation of a Nazi-like movement in a high school setting, and Philip Zimbardo's prison simulation at Stanford University.[20] In the latter a group of student volunteers were randomly divided into guards and prisoners. In only six days, the guards became aggressive and abusive, the prisoners passive and subservient. Afterward many expressed surprise that they were capable of such behavior. Both experiments again demonstrated that ordinary people are capable of far greater evil than might have been expected. Both also incorporated a social factor excluded from Milgram's individual-centered design: the influence of group pressure and group pride. These experiments are, of course, merely simulations. Peck and Lifton take us into the real world of evil to test how far these experimental findings hold.

My Lai

In the spring of 1972 Peck was appointed by the surgeon general of the Army to chair a committee investigating the My Lai massacre for the purpose of drawing up a research proposal concerning its psychological causes. The committee's proposal was rejected by the army as potentially embarrassing to the administration, but in *People of the Lie* Peck has reported his findings as a case study for understanding the phenomenon of group evil. Because the recommended research was never undertaken, Peck acknowledges that his conclusions are unavoidably somewhat speculative.

The event in question may be summarized as follows. On March 16, 1968, Task Force Barker, consisting of five hundred hastily-trained men who had been frustrated in their efforts to engage an enemy that had been booby-trapping them, eagerly began a "search-and-destroy" mission into a collection of hamlets known as My Lai. The task force anticipated that in this Vietcong stronghold it would be difficult to distinguish between guerrilla fighters and their civilian supporters.

When C Company entered the cluster of hamlets, they found only unarmed women, children, and old men. The troops of C Company proceeded to kill between five hundred and six hundred of these unarmed civilians. Some, including children, were shot as they attempted to run. Others were cut down in their huts by indiscriminate rifle fire. The largest number were herded together in groups of twenty to forty and slaughtered with hand grenades and machine gun fire.

The massacre continued throughout the morning, witnessed by approximately two hundred persons. Only one tried to stop the slaughter, a helicopter pilot who landed after discerning what was happening from the air. His pleas went unheeded, even when he radioed word to his commanding officers. Although failure to report a crime is itself a crime, My Lai went unreported for a year, until a soldier heard about the massacre in casual conversation and wrote to several congressional representatives following his discharge.

Peck states the problem that this atrocity and its cover-up present to us: "How is it that approximately five hundred men, the majority of whom were undoubtedly not evil as individuals, could all have participated in an act as monstrously evil as that at My Lai?"[21]

What led individuals to behave as they did, Peck concludes, was no single cause, but a manifold of more than a dozen factors, all well-known to social psychologists. Yet even the combined weight of all these pressures, he insists, is not sufficient to excuse individual soldiers from personal responsibility for their actions. "Even the helicopter pilot," he asserts, "can be blamed for not reporting what he saw beyond the first echelon of authority over him."[22] Having emphasized personal accountability, Peck then proceeds to take us up "the ladder of collective responsibility," from individual to task force to the entire nation.

At the most basic level is the factor of *regression under stress.* Soldiers under pressure of combat revert to less mature behavior, Peck states, and immature persons are more prone to commit evil acts. Regression also produces increased *dependence on leadership,* so that under battle conditions, troops are more likely to obey orders (good or bad) without question. In addition, combat induces *"psychic numbing,"* as constant exposure to blood and gore desensitizes combatants to the horror. "When it no longer bothers us to see mangled bodies, it will no longer bother us to mangle them ourselves."[23]

At the group level an *esprit de corps* develops, leading individuals to go along with the crowd. When group-spirit is stung by failure, it becomes dangerous. *Wounded pride* lashes out, producing an atmosphere that is conducive to atrocities. Not only does one's own group become more homogeneous; so does the perception of one's opponent. Warfare leads to *"enemy creation":* the stereotyping and scapegoating of one's foe. It is easier to destroy people who are inferior and blameworthy. Communism, Americans believed, is an evil force that must be opposed everywhere and by any means necessary.[24] Racism made that duty even easier, for "wasting gooks" was no "big deal."[25]

An additional factor making killing easier is *specialization.* The United States, like every other country, recruits and trains soldiers to do its dirty work. Task Force Barker was created for one special purpose: "search and destroy," and that's what it did. Peck claims that there is also a degree of self-selection in a combat unit, as in any specialized group, so that its personnel will be those least uncomfortable with the specialty of killing.

Specialization also diffuses responsibility, so that it is difficult to hold any one person accountable.

On the national level, two factors contributing to evil are *narcissism* and *laziness.* In earlier chapters of *People of the Lie,* Peck identified these same two factors as key motivators toward individual evil. Narcissism he defines as "self-absorption," "overweening pride," the "arrogant self-image of perfection."[26] Thus what Senator Fulbright called "the arrogance of power," Peck identifies as "malignant national narcissism," the American self-image of perfection.[27] The United States couldn't be wrong. What the Vietnamese themselves think is unimportant; we know what's best for them.

During the war, such nationalistic arrogance was combined with astonishing ignorance about Vietnam. Peck polled troops on their way to battle to find out what they knew about Vietnam and the war. The enlisted men knew nothing, he reports, and what little some officers knew, they had learned through military indoctrination. He discovered a similar ignorance of Vietnamese history among Department of Defense civilians who directed the war.[28] As the folly of U.S. policy began to be exposed, the government (in typical narcissistic fashion) covered up by lying, as in the padded "body counts" and the fraudulent "Gulf of Tonkin Incident," and escalated the war to prove its actions right.[29] It is easier to go on doing what you've been doing than to acknowledge the mistake and undertake the agony of change, says Peck. That's what he means by laziness: clinging to "old maps" and obsolete attitudes.[30]

Americans were for the most part unwitting villains, Peck acknowledges, but how could a whole nation be unwitting? "As a people," he states, "we were too lazy to learn and too arrogant to think we needed to learn.... With our laziness and narcissism feeding each other, we marched off to impose our will on the Vietnamese people by bloodshed with practically no idea of what was involved."[31] Thus laziness and narcissism were twin progenitors of the evil that broke out at My Lai.[32]

How could so many individuals have participated in such a monstrous evil as My Lai? Not because they were evil persons, says Peck, and not because they were given an evil order. It can only be explained by taking into consideration the whole constellation of pressures — psychological, social, and cultural, ranging from regression under stress all the way up to national narcissism and laziness — pressures pushing the troops of C Company toward indiscriminate killing, with very little to restrain them under battle conditions. Peck's systemic approach is especially helpful in showing how a multiplicity of factors, no one of which is a sufficient condition, can interact to produce an explosion of evil. Yet for Peck none of that excuses what any individual did, for personal freedom and moral responsibility remain, in spite of all the forces moving the soldiers of C Company toward atrocity.

In preceding chapters of *People of the Lie,* Peck presented arguments for the reality of "evil persons" and Satanic possession. In regard to the latter, he wrote, "I now know Satan is real. I have met it."[33] The surprising thing, then, is that Peck attributes the admittedly greater danger of group evil neither to Satan nor to evil persons. The dynamics of group evil are purely human in Peck's analysis, a combination of psychological, social, and moral factors. It is a very persuasive model of the way normal human beings could participate in an atrocity like My Lai, and apparently Peck feels no need to search beyond those human factors. Even if one accepts that model, however, it is still a long distance from an atrocity that lasted a few hours to the monstrosity of Auschwitz, which extended over years.

Nazi Doctors

Lifton's study of Nazi doctors and the psychology of genocide began when an editor of one of Lifton's earlier books invited him to examine some recently acquired documents concerning Dr. Josef Mengele and the practice of medicine in Auschwitz. The documents quickly disclosed the central role played by Nazi physicians in the extermination camps. Certainly this was not the first time that doctors had contributed to evil, but here a threshold was crossed into genocide, justified and supervised by the medical profession in a strange reversal of healing and killing.[34] How that came about, and what generalizations concerning human evil can be drawn therefrom, is the purpose of *Nazi Doctors,* a study based on extensive interviews of death-camp physicians and survivors.[35]

During World War II six million Jews were systematically exterminated in a series of camps built expressly for that purpose by Nazi Germany. One million of those died in Auschwitz, a

name that has come to stand for the entire genocidal project
of the Holocaust. When Auschwitz was operating at its peak
in 1944, ten thousand persons a day were gassed and cremated
there, all under the direction of German SS physicians.[36]

How was that possible for human beings, let alone physicians
sworn to the Hippocratic oath? An Auschwitz survivor put the
question to Lifton this way: "Were they *beasts* when they did
what they did? Or were they *human beings?*" It is a legitimate
question, for some have attributed the mass murder to sadistic
guards, or to "monsters" like the notorious Dr. Josef Mengele, or
to the demonic Führer, Adolf Hitler. Lifton's reply was that the
Nazi doctors were ordinary humans beings, not inherently evil,
nor sadistic, nor demonic. Auschwitz, he said, "was a product
of specifically *human* ingenuity and cruelty."

"But it is *demonic* that they were *not* demonic," objected
the survivor, pointing out through that paradoxical expression
how much more difficult it is to come to terms with the Holocaust morally if we cannot dismiss its perpetrators as "monsters"
who are quite different from ourselves. "The disturbing psychological truth," Lifton comments, is that "ordinary people can
commit demonic acts," an observation reiterated many times
through the book.

Lifton's interrogator had one more question. "How did they
become killers?"[37] That, Lifton tells the reader, is the question
his book is written to address. More specifically, "My goal in
this study is to uncover psychological conditions conducive to
evil."[38] In pursuing that goal, Lifton intends to avoid two pit-
falls. The first is the *hubris* of exceeding the limits of human
understanding. A survivor had forewarned him, "The professor
would like to understand what is not understandable."[39] The
second pitfall is reductionism: substituting psychological explanation for moral judgment. "By combining psychological and
moral considerations," Lifton claims, "one can better understand the nature of the evil and the motivations of the men."[40]

How, then, did the SS doctors become killers? Like Peck,
Lifton identifies a long list of causes that converged to produce
Auschwitz. They may, however, be clustered under three major
headings: (1) the Nazi ideology of "applied biology," (2) the
machine-like bureaucracy, which institutionalized that vision
through a series of incremental steps, until the threshold of genocide was crossed, and (3) psychological mechanisms, especially

"doubling," which made it possible for ordinary people to engage in mass murder. The three are profoundly interrelated and difficult to separate, even for purposes of discussion.

National Socialism as "Applied Biology"

"National Socialism is nothing but applied biology," said Rudolf Hess.[41] Combining a romanticized version of Darwin's "natural selection" with Mendel's genetics, Nazi ideology called for the development of a Master Race. To accomplish this, Himmler advocated "annihilation of the Jewish people," together with a program "to select the Nordic-Germanic blood" for the purpose of enhancing "the creative, heroic and life-preserving qualities of our people."[42] This plan to eliminate "life unworthy of life" was justified by a medical metaphor. The sickness of the German nation, manifest in Germany's defeat in World War I and the decade of malaise following, was caused by pollution of the Aryan race. The therapy needed to restore health to the nation was the purging of that impurity.

Such a subordination of individual to national health was consistent with Hitler's contrast between the "insignificance of the individual" and "the visible immortality of the Nation."[43] If, then, the health of the body required excision of some cells, a good surgeon would not hesitate. "Our task here is surgical," said Goebbels, "...drastic incisions, or some day Europe will perish of the Jewish disease."[44] With this emphasis on the corporate health of the *Volk* (people), the Nazis enlisted the support of the medical profession for its program of killing as a "therapeutic imperative." Forty-five percent of physicians became party members, the largest percentage of any professional group.[45]

Implementation of such a program required "heroic hardness," a value celebrated in Nazi ideology. A good soldier must be ready to sacrifice not only his own life but the lives of any who stand in the way of the *Volk*. There is no place for tender emotions like sympathy (especially for the weak, who deserve to be eliminated). Instead, one must think with "cold logic," Himmler said. Indeed, from Hitler's premises, "cold logic" leads ineluctably to killing. "Hardness" means not shrinking back from the unpleasant duties which that entails.

"We are meaning-hungry creatures," says Lifton. "We live

on images of meaning."[46] A Germany hungry for transcendent meaning found it in the Nazi vision:

> As [Hitler] invoked principles of "'honor,' 'fatherland,' '*Volk,*' 'loyalty,' and 'sacrifice,' his German hearers... hung on them as upon the message of a savior." For each of these words represented a transcendent principle, a means of offering the self to an ultimate realm that provided a sense of immortality bordering on omnipotence.[47]

By blaming the victims and calling for their eradication, this immortalizing vision provided plenty of ammunition for killing.

Institutionalizing the Vision

The Nazi ideology was institutionalized step by step through a sequence of five programs, each gradually expanded, each replete with "slippery-slope" compromises, each taking the Third Reich a step closer to genocide.[48] First came coercive sterilization, implemented less than six months after Hitler came to power. Between 1933 and 1936, physicians sterilized between 200,000 and 350,000 persons: the mentally ill, mentally handicapped, those with hereditary defects, and the like.[49] The second step was "mercy killing" of defective children within the hospitals where they were patients. Adult "euthanasia" came next.[50] The victims, mostly patients in mental hospitals, were transported to killing centers, where death was administered by carbon monoxide poisoning in specially-constructed "shower rooms." Both types of "euthanasia" were well underway by the outbreak of the war in 1939. The fourth step was the use of these same centers to exterminate "impaired" inmates of concentration camps.

With these experiments in mass murder as rehearsal and prefiguration, the threshold to genocide was crossed. Surprisingly, this did not come about as the result of a clear command from above. In Lifton's reconstruction, there was "an evolving genocidal mentality," in which initiatives from below and indirect messages from above converged on a point of collective understanding, involving "a vast number of people working in concert as perpetrators."[51] "Collective understanding quickly becomes collective will as perpetrators join in the process on the basis of what is expected of them, calling forth prior inclination and adaptive doubling."[52] Thus in Lifton's reading of the events, all of the factors conducive to evil came together in the spring of 1941 to create a critical mass that exploded in the evil of genocide. Himmler stated the consensus: "All Jews within our grasp are to be destroyed without exception, now, during the war."[53] For this purpose Auschwitz and other extermination camps were built, carrying over from the prior programs many of the same procedures and technology, and even some of the same personnel and equipment.

Medical professionals were involved at all levels of these five projects. Physicians performed the sterilizations and delivered the lethal injections. "The syringe belongs in the hand of a physician," said a leader of the "euthanasia" program.[54] In Auschwitz SS doctors performed large-scale "selections" as the transports arrived, consigning directly to the gas chamber as much as 80 percent of a trainload of Jews. They also performed further selections within the camp, supervised the gassing and pronounced death, signed false death certificates, and advised on cremation procedures.[55] "Medical activity in Auschwitz," said a Nazi doctor, "consisted only of selecting people for the gas chamber."[56] No medical expertise was needed to perform that function, but placing doctors in charge maintained the myth of therapeutic killing and gave the impression that "an exact medical judgment had been made."[57]

Extensive use of medical personnel and medical-sounding procedures resulted in a bureaucracy of deception. The deception was as much for the physicians themselves as for the victims and the public. For example, a "euthanasia expert" explained that medical examinations before sending victims to the gas chamber "served mainly to calm the conscience of the doctor who has to carry out the killing."[58] Even in Auschwitz an elaborate "as if" game was played. Doctors in white coats "selected" persons for "special treatment" (death), sending them to "showers" for "disinfection," where they received Zyklon-B gas, delivered in a truck marked with a red cross and administered by "disinfectors." The elaborate deception in these programs was deemed necessary because victims, perpetrators, and the public were not yet ready for the *avant garde* program of therapeutic killing devised by the scientific and moral elite of the Third Reich.

The bureaucratic structure also served to fragment responsibility through specialization, so that each could deny personal blame. In Auschwitz a medical corpsman (the "disinfector") did the actual killing, the corpses were seen only by the doctor in charge of the gas chamber, and everything was done in obedience to the Führer's orders. Thus each physician could say, "It is not I who kill."[59] The result was a strange paradox of omnipotence and impotence: "the sense of omnipotent control over the lives and deaths of prisoners and the seemingly opposite sense of impotence, of being a powerless cog in a vast machine controlled by unseen others."[60] The camp doctors were resigned to participation in mass killing as an unalterable fact of their existence: "I'm here. I cannot get out. I have to make the best of it."[61]

Psychological Patterns Conducive to Evil: Doubling

"Doubling," a concept that emerged from Lifton's research, is the major new idea presented in *Nazi Doctors.* Lifton also describes more than a dozen additional psychological patterns, especially "psychic numbing," which contributed to Nazi genocide and are conducive to human evil generally.

Lifton claims that doubling is "the key to understanding how Nazi doctors came to do the work of Auschwitz." Beyond that, it is "an overall key to human evil."[62] Doubling may be defined as the division of the self into two relatively autonomous selves in order to survive under extreme conditions, typically death-saturated environments such as Auschwitz.[63] The second self ("Auschwitz self" in Lifton's terminology) is needed to perform "the dirty work" necessary for survival — deeds that the original self could not perform because of their incompatibility with that person's self-image and values. Hence the two "selves" differ from each other in behavior and values, enough to give the appearance of being "two different people."[64]

The process of doubling is not in itself bad, in Lifton's view. As an adaptation to an extreme situation, it may be the only way to survive. Lifton suggests that doubling is a healthy response for soldiers in combat or prisoners in a death camp, a kind of "lesser of two evils" adaptation to an extremely threatening situation. "Clearly, the 'opposing self' can be life enhancing," Lifton acknowledges. "But under certain conditions it can embrace evil with an extreme lack of restraint."[65] Thus doubling, while not in itself a malignant process, opens up tremendous potential for evil when the conditions are ripe for it. Although in Lifton's view humans are not inherently evil, doubling is the psychological mechanism that makes them potentially capable of it under certain conditions.

Those conditions prevailed in Auschwitz. It was "a different planet," requiring "a different kind of mentality," in which the rules of normal society were totally reversed.[66]

> Dr. B. observed that each SS doctor could call forth two radically different psychological constellations within the self: one based on "values generally accepted" and the education and background of a "normal person"; the other based on "this [Nazi-Auschwitz] ideology with values quite different from those generally accepted."[67]

The two "selves" nevertheless remained significantly related to each other by mutual need. The prior self needed the Auschwitz self to perform murderous deeds it could not do, and the Auschwitz self needed the prior self to be able think of itself as humane physician, husband, and father.[68] Guilt was avoided by transferring conscience to the Auschwitz self, where it functioned within the framework of death-camp values like duty, group loyalty, heroic hardness. "The feeling was something like: 'Anything I do on planet Auschwitz doesn't count on planet earth.'"[69] This transfer was not a denial of reality (for the Nazi doctor knew he was participating in killing), but it did alter the *meaning* of that reality. Selecting was not murder, but purifying the race, protecting public health in the camp, or providing humane death for persons already condemned.

The birthing of the Auschwitz self began with a doctor's first selection, which was a baptism into the Auschwitz self through death immersion. It was a ritual ordeal to test "hardness" and an initiation solidifying in "blood cement" the kinship to colleagues, not unlike initiations into "gangs" of criminal organizations. "Selections thus ritualized the practice of murder and the acceptance of evil, both made possible by the increasing immersion of the Auschwitz self in the healing-killing paradox."[70] Within a matter of days after a doctor's arrival at the camp, selections became "normal duty," "a regular job."[71] From that point on the Auschwitz self assumed dominance of day-to-day life, restricting the prior self to odd moments and family visits.[72] After the war, however, the prior self reasserted dominance, so that only vestiges of the Auschwitz self remained. This completed the cycle, frequently noted by Lifton, from pre-Nazi healing physician to Nazi killing physician to post-Nazi healing physician.

Numerous other psychological patterns functioned together with doubling. In order for the Nazi doctors to carry out their murderous duty, it was necessary for them to become radically desensitized through the process of *psychic numbing,* defined by Lifton as "diminished capacity or inclination to feel."[73] Screening out excess stimuli is an everyday psychological need, but it becomes extreme in death-saturated situations, blocking out feelings of empathy and guilt. In fact, Lifton believes that "it is probably impossible to kill another human being without numbing oneself toward that victim."[74] Through numbing, the Nazi doctor "no longer experienced [Jews] as beings who affected him — that is, as human beings."[75] They simply didn't count. Such numbing can be willed, Lifton claims, and it can be increased by continuous immersion in a deadly environment. After the first selection or two, "one had, in effect, made a pledge to stay numbed."[76]

Numbing and doubling were reinforced by a number of other psychological patterns operative in the death camps. *Heavy drinking* served to deaden responses as well as facilitate male bonding with colleagues. *Technicizing* and *distancing* facilitated numbing in the same way that B-52 bomber crews were insulated from their victims in Vietnam.[77] The invention of the gas chamber was a technical breakthrough that eliminated the trauma of face-to-face shooting, a major psychological obstacle in the early stages of Nazi genocide. *Dampening of language* deluded participants concerning the reality of their deeds. "Special treatment," "selection," and "resettlement" were euphemisms for murder, and "Final Solution" was a code word for genocide.[78] Finally, *construction of meaning,* by which positive value was conferred on Auschwitz, was "part of a universal proclivity toward constructing good motives while participating in evil behavior." This process often included *blaming the victim* as justification for the Final Solution. "Man can make meaning of anything," Lifton concludes.[79] All these factors, he asserts, are generalizable to other situations of potential evil.[80]

The Human Face of Evil

An Auschwitz survivor, while watching the Eichmann trial on television, sensed a disturbing similarity between Eichmann and his Israeli prosecutor. She eventually recognized the similarity as a disclosure of the truth that "others, her own people, she herself, could, under certain conditions, also be capable of evil behavior."[81] After his many interviews, Lifton arrived at the same conclusion. "Most of what Nazi doctors did would be within the potential capability — at least under certain conditions — of most doctors and most people."[82] *Nazi Doctors* juxtaposes two disturbing realities: on the one hand there are the evil deeds, the horror and scope of which stagger the imagination, perpetrated daily by doctors in Auschwitz; on the other hand there are the all-too-human faces of these same doctors, as revealed in Lifton's interviews — faces in which the reader's own image is mirrored.

This does not mean that "we are all Nazis." Such a generalization, Lifton protests, would gloss over the crucial distinction between potential and actual evil. He notes that for the most part, humans do not act on the universal potential for murder and genocide. Lifton claims that "the formation of an evil self" requires a moral choice.[83]

To live out the doubling and call forth the evil is a moral choice for which one is responsible, whatever the level of consciousness involved. By means of doubling, Nazi doctors made a Faustian choice for evil.[84]

It is at this point that Lifton's refusal to reduce moral judgment to psychological explanation has its greatest significance. Lifton, no less than Peck, insists that actualizing the human potential for evil is always a choice and cannot be blamed on factors beyond one's control.

Yet by adding the qualifying phrase "under certain conditions" to his generalization concerning the human potential for evil, Lifton also recognizes "the extraordinary power of the environment to issue a 'call' to genocide."[85] Indeed, that "call" to genocide can be so powerful as to make the choice "virtually certain."

> Nazi doctors found themselves in a psychological climate
> where they were virtually certain to choose evil; they were
> propelled, that is, toward murder.[86]

> If the destructive ideological and behavioral pressures are
> sufficiently great, virtually any professional self may be sus-
> ceptible to moving in genocidal directions.[87]

In his paradoxical insistence that a virtually certain choice is
nevertheless one's moral responsibility, Lifton is emphasizing
the extreme difficulty of resisting social pressures toward evil.

An additional paradox is involved in Lifton's assertion that
one is morally responsible for choices "whatever the level of
consciousness involved." It seems that awareness of evil and
even of one's own decision for evil may be less than fully con-
scious, resident in some twilight zone of semi-awareness. For
instance, concerning "the atmosphere of genocide" he writes,

> It becomes a kind of "middle knowledge" — something
> one knows and does not know, or acts upon without clearly
> knowing, or knows and does not act upon. It is a combina-
> tion of knowledge and numbing, but the knowledge seeps
> through.[88]

Here, too, moral choice is "a responsibility in no way abro-
gated by the fact that much doubling takes place outside of
awareness."[89] The paradoxes of "unconscious choice," and "virtually certain choice," both of which can also be found in Peck,
highlight the difficulty of moral responsibility and reveal the
logic of such ready rationalizations as "I didn't know," or "I
had no choice."

Although evil is powerful enough virtually to overwhelm human freedom, Lifton does not postulate any superhuman power
of evil. It is true that evil, in Lifton's model, is far more for-
midable than the simple sum of individual human choices. In
this sense evil power does indeed become transpersonal, but it
is lodged in human social creations such as ideologies, movements, and institutions.

Theologically, human creativity is a dimension of the human
image of God and therefore good, and so are its cultural and social products, which have positive potential for enhancing hu-

man life and safeguarding freedom. But cultural creations and social structures also have frightening potential for destruction, as *Nazi Doctors* thoroughly documents. Auschwitz, too, "was a product of specifically human ingenuity."[90] Hence what Lifton says regarding the human self — "evil is neither inherent in the self nor foreign to it" — could be said about all the key ingredients in the production of evil: human nature, human freedom, the potential for doubling, ideologies, and social institutions. The potential for evil as well as good in each of these elements, especially in combination, is the opening through which evil enters the world.

Many of Lifton's findings in *Nazi Doctors* are corroborated in a recently published study of Greek torturers.[91] After examining testimony taken during the 1975 Athens trials of former army torturers, Janice T. Gibson and Mika Haritos-Fatouros conducted in-depth interviews with sixteen of them. Like the Nazi doctors, all sixteen were leading normal lives at the time they were interviewed, and none had been involved in delinquent or disturbed behavior prior to military service. They had "normal personalities"; in fact, the researchers speculate that "one probably cannot train a deranged sadist to be an effective torturer or killer." Furthermore, the torturers, like Lifton's doctors and Zimbardo's prison guards, were abusive only within prison walls. Outside they were decent husbands and fathers. All were draftees who had been screened for strength, intelligence, and "appropriate" political beliefs (anticommunism), then assigned to units that specialized in torture.

After a brutal initiation, they underwent continued harassment and punishment that kept them in constant fear and that numbed their sensitivity to what they were doing. At the same time, their trainers instilled elitist attitudes that let them know they were different from the "outside world." They were given special privileges, so that carrot and stick were held in balance. Meanwhile their anticommunist indoctrination proceeded; they came to believe that their prisoners were "worms" who deserved to be "crushed." Step by step they were introduced to torture. First they brought food to cells, then observed torture, then were instructed to "give some blows," then participated in group beatings. Finally they were put in charge of torturing. This last step was taken without advance notice, to deprive them of time to think about it. Thus were ordinary citizens turned into efficient torturers. Reiterating the findings of Milgram, Zimbardo, Peck, and Lifton, the researchers conclude, "Any of us, in a similar situation, might be capable of the same cruelty."[92]

Our survey has unearthed a massive array of factors contributing to the large-scale social evils that we have had under consideration. No one of these by itself is a sufficient cause of such evil, but when a large number of them operate together in concert, evil can explode, and ordinary people will be caught up in it. Although the list of such factors is extensive, they may be clustered under five headings: (1) an *ideology* that, at least by implication, supports, encourages, and justifies the evil project; (2) *institutionalization* of that project (preferably one small step at a time) in such a way that it develops its own momentum and authority while fragmenting individual responsibility for decisions; (3) *group elitism and pride,* binding members together, pressuring them to conform, and distancing them from a stereotyped and devalued "enemy"; (4) *psychological mechanisms to overcome resistance,* including obedience, doubling, and numbing, without which participation in social evil would scarcely be possible for normal human beings, and such other mechanisms as regression under stress, distancing, and blaming the victim; (5) *individual decision* to participate. All five of these must be operative to some degree, I would argue, in order for massive social evil to happen, and efforts to resist or build safeguards against social evil would have to address these five.

"We Have Met the Enemy..."

Earlier we posed the question whether human choices alone could adequately account for the massive evil let loose in this century, or whether the whirlwind of demonic forces we have witnessed points to some superhuman power, alien to the human spirit, that holds us in thrall. Peck and Lifton have helped us to see that both are simultaneously true. They have shown how a sequence of human decisions can create a Juggernaut that takes on a life of its own, destroying everything in its path and overwhelming the freedom even of those who created it. It is like drug addiction, initiated in a free decision but enslaving its user, even while the addict believes he or she is still in charge.

The potential for evil in a dynamic social movement does not lie solely in its effectiveness in compelling compliance. More insidious than its power to coerce is its power to enthrall. It captivates human imagination with an immortalizing vision and exploits human weaknesses for its own aggrandizement. The strange paradox of omnipotence and impotence is enacted, as its followers willingly give over their limited powers in exchange for participation in omnipotence. Unrestrained, the incarnated vision can become a demonic nightmare, destroying all that stands in its way until, like Nazism in Europe or Jonestown in Guyana, it destroys even itself in a *Götterdämmerung,* a twilight of the gods.

"Gods" points us to the domain in which this dynamic operates, for what we have been describing is religious fervor in devotion to a false god, the phenomenon that the Hebrew prophets knew as idolatry. Especially relevant is the text in which Isaiah ridicules the man who cuts down a tree, uses half of it to build a fire for food and warmth, and with the remainder creates a "god":

> And the rest of it he makes into a god, his idol; and falls down to it and worships it; he prays to it and says, "Deliver me, for thou art my god!"
> They know not, nor do they discern, for he has shut their eyes, so that they cannot see, and their minds, so that they cannot understand.... He feeds on ashes; a deluded mind has led him astray, and he cannot deliver himself or say, "Is there not a lie in my right hand?" (Isa. 44:17–20)

It is a chillingly accurate description of Nazism, from the idol created to bring deliverance to the self-deluded "not-knowing" that cannot extricate itself from the lie. If the idol of Americanism is less readily discerned in Isaiah's prophecy, the reason may be, as the text states and Peck observes, that our idol has blinded our minds.

In the New Testament the nearest equivalent to "idols" are "Principalities and Powers," which are creations of God and therefore good.[93] They were created to be God's agents, but some have "fallen." A "power" is always incarnate in some worldly structure, such as a government, institution, or church, but a power's inner or spiritual dimension is as important as its outer embodiment. "Principality" is a case in point. In the New Testament, "principality" sometimes refers to a transcendent

power operative in government and sometimes to the earthly
rule that is its manifestation, but always both are presupposed.
The two aspects cannot be separated, for the spiritual dimension is the inner essence of the outer form. By way of analogy,
Walter Wink suggests "team spirit," a reality powerful enough
to win games, yet without any separate existence apart from the
team or the season of play.[94]

Many of the powers mentioned in the New Testament have
become enemies of God. Wink interprets this "fall" of the powers in terms of idolatry. "When a particular Power becomes
idolatrous, placing itself above God's purpose for the good of
the whole, then that power becomes demonic."[95] Satan is such a
power, the demonic essence of corporate structures that have become idolatrous. " 'Satan,' " says Wink, "is the actual power that
congeals around collective idolatry, injustice, or inhumanity."[96]
Fundamentalism's error, he claims, is to interpret Satan and the
demons too literally and too individualistically, thereby over-
looking the truly satanic evils of racism and oppression, ecolog-
ical pollution and the nuclear arms race. Liberalism's error is
to discard that image altogether, leaving us without language to
point to the reality of demonic evil. We need "the power of the
Satan-image," he argues, "*not* as an explanation of evil — for
Satan explains nothing — but as a way of keeping its irreducible
malignancy before our eyes."[97]

This understanding of New Testament "powers" becomes
particularly relevant to Lifton's analysis when Wink quotes a
German pastor regarding the Nazi era:

> You cannot understand what has happened in Germany
> unless you understand that we were possessed by demonic
> powers. I do not say this to excuse ourselves, because *we
> let ourselves be possessed.*

Those demonic powers, Wink adds, were not "discarnate spiri-
tual beings in the air," but *"the actual spirituality of Nazism."*[98]
The fit between Wink's interpretation of "powers" in the New
Testament and Lifton's analysis of the dynamics of evil in the
Third Reich is striking.

The conclusion to which our inquiry has brought us is that
demonic evil is a reality perilous to ignore, but that we need not
look beyond human processes to discern its source. There are,

to be sure, transpersonal structures of evil so powerful that they can virtually overwhelm any individual when the conditions are ripe, and all too often in this century cultural, social, and psychological dynamics have conspired to produce just such conditions. Yet those forces have their origins in human decisions. We cannot take refuge in the excuse of Flip Wilson's character Geraldine: "The devil made me do it." At the same time, this has not pushed us to the misanthropic conclusion that all of us are inherently evil; nor has it lifted from us the moral responsibility for what has happened and may yet happen. Instead, it leads us to acknowledge our potential not only to do evil but to become evil; it warns us of the demonic potential of our ideologies, social structures, and psychological patterns; it humbles us to seek God's forgiveness for the human evil perpetrated in this century; and it inspires us to pray for God's guidance and empowerment to build safeguards against its repetition in the next.

Chapter 5

"My God, My God . . . ": Holy Passion and Compassion

Our inquiry thus far has focused on the twin realities of suffering and evil, viewed against the backdrop of faith in God. Now it is time to reverse foreground and background to consider more directly who God is for us, how God relates to the human cry of affliction, and the radical rethinking this is receiving in the twentieth century.

Let us begin with a brief working definition of God that has been around a long time, first proposed by St. Anselm in the eleventh century: "We believe that thou art a being, than which nothing greater can be conceived."[1] By this definition Anselm intends us to understand that God is not just the greatest being that actually exists; God is the greatest that anyone could even *imagine,* in this world or in any possible world. Other terms that have been used to express this idea of God are "perfect being" and "infinite being." The various divine attributes, then, are statements of what is essential to a perfect or infinite being, to "that than which none greater can be conceived." We have already seen that omnipotence and perfect goodness are two of these attributes. We have also discovered that these terms are not unambiguous, but depend on the context in which goodness and power are themselves understood. The same is true of the concept of perfection. Much of this century's reconsideration of the doctrine of God comes from changes in our understanding of these basic ideas. Before examining the impact of contemporary thinking, however, let us identify briefly the biblical and classical roots of these terms.

Biblical Roots

Unlike the abstract, conceptual thinking of Greek philosophy and Western theology generally, biblical thinking is concrete and imagistic, and so our mode of inquiry to some degree forces biblical patterns into unfamiliar categories. Nevertheless, it is not difficult to find the biblical roots of divine omnipotence and benevolence. The generic Semitic name for God is *"El,"* which means "power." *"El Shaddai,"* usually translated as "God Almighty," appears frequently in Genesis, Exodus, and Job. In the very first verses of scripture we learn of a God so powerful as to create by a mere word. "And God said, 'Let there be...,' and it was so!" Following creation comes the pronouncement, "It was good." God is as God does, so from the beginning we have a powerful and good God. The theme of God's power is reiterated over and over in the Hebrew scriptures, especially in the Psalms. Psalm 89:8 can be taken as representative: "O Lord God of hosts, who is mighty as thou art, O Lord, with thy faithfulness round about thee?"

In the book of Job, *"El Shaddai"* (often translated simply as "Lord") is used thirty-five times, probably to emphasize divine omnipotence. In chapter 38, near the end of the book, God wields that power like a club in reply to Job's constant complaints and insistent appeals for an answer to his suffering. God's voice speaks to Job from the whirlwind, shouting a series of rhetorical questions:

4 Were you there when I made the world?
  If you know so much, tell me about it.
5 Who decided how large it would be?
  Who stretched the measuring lines over it?
  Do you know all the answers?...
12 Job, have you ever in all your life
  commanded a day to dawn?...
18 Have you any idea how big the world is?
  Answer me if you know. (Job 38:4–18 TEV)

And so on, for four long chapters. No reason for Job's afflictions is actually given, only an overwhelming display of raw power, a put-down of Job's puny questions. Such a show of sheer force is rather uncharacteristic of the biblical God. It may well be a parody of divine power by the author of Job, who satirizes so many of the then-current answers to the problem of suffering. German theologian Dorothee Sölle comments, "Job relies on the God who led his people out of suffering in Egypt. The God whom he encounters is merely another Pharaoh."[2]

Sölle's remark reminds us that in the Bible God's power is normally exercised in service of God's justice, especially in defense of the weak and the helpless. The paradigm for that is the Exodus. "I have seen the affliction of my people who are in Egypt, and have heard their cry because of their taskmasters; I know their sufferings, and I have come down to deliver them from the hand of the Egyptians" (Exod. 3:7-8). Hebrew faith marks its true beginning from the moment when the Lord God took mercy on the oppressed Hebrews and redeemed them out of slavery. God's gracious goodness is identified with the empowerment of God's people and with their liberation from bondage. That grace is, as the hymn declares, "amazing": it is surprising and unexpected. Yet it is also dependable, not whimsical or capricious. Over and over again the Psalms speak of God's "steadfast love." Psalm 103, hearkening back to the Exodus, declares:

> 6 The Lord works vindication and justice for all who are oppressed....
> 8 The Lord is merciful and gracious, slow to anger and abounding in steadfast love.

Altogether the term "steadfast love" occurs four times in this psalm. Psalm 89, from which the verse extolling God's power was taken, also celebrates God's steadfast love:

> 1 I will sing of thy steadfast love, O Lord, for ever; with my mouth I will proclaim thy faithfulness to all generations.
> 2 For thy steadfast love was established for ever, thy faithfulness is firm as the heavens.

Yet if God's steadfast love is liberating, it is also binding, for the covenant at Sinai follows immediately on the Exodus. Justice and mercy are constantly yoked as the marks of the covenant. "What does the Lord require of you," asks Micah, "but to do justice, to love kindness, and to walk humbly with your God?" (Micah 6:8).

The covenant not only binds liberated Israel to its God, but God to "my people." That divine binding to Israel is expressed over and over again in psalms praising God's faithfulness, as is evident in the verses from Psalm 89 previously cited. In faithfulness to the covenant, God is now committed, and that commitment means that there are some things God will not do, for God has given the divine word of promise. Thus in the Hebrew scripture God's power is not independent of God's steadfast and faithful love but is used in its furtherance, often to empower the powerless.

The New Testament extends this understanding of God and gives it its own unique turn. The power of God includes power to heal the sick, expel demons, raise the dead, and bring in God's Reign. God's liberating action in the Exodus is echoed in the liberation proclaimed by Jesus at Nazareth (Luke 4:18–21) and in the redemption from bondage to sin and death that comes through his cross and resurrection. The justice of God is transcended in the prodigality of God's grace, expressed in the three parables of the lost coin, the lost sheep, and the lost son, spoken in the context of Jesus' shocking act of eating with tax-collectors and sinners (Luke 15). The "steadfast love" of God lauded by the psalmist is reflected in the New Testament's paeans to God's love, culminating in John's bold claim that "God *is* love" (1 John 4:8).

Classical Theism

In these ways the scripture shaped the Judeo-Christian understanding of God. By the beginning of the Christian era, however, both Judaism and Christianity had moved out of Palestine into the surrounding Hellenistic world, and both were deeply affected by the mindset of classical antiquity. The Greeks had their ideas of God too, which were similar enough to biblical thinking to have an impact on it, yet distinct enough to turn theology in new directions. The Greek concept of "perfect being" does not sound radically different from the biblical view of God, but Hellenistic culture had its own assumptions about what "perfection" meant. The word "perfect" comes from the Latin verb meaning "to finish" or "complete." A "perfect being," then, is one that is complete in all respects. All possibilities have been realized, all potentialities actualized; hence a perfect being lacks nothing and needs nothing.

Following this line of thinking, the church declared as dogma that God neither lacked nor needed anything. This assertion has some surprising implications. For instance, a perfect being cannot possibly change, for any change from perfection could only be toward imperfection, which would contradict God's essential nature. Hence God is by definition unchanging, the "*unmoved* mover," as Aristotle said. This is the doctrine of divine *immutability.*

Immutability in turn implies *impassibility,* the doctrine that God is "without passion," devoid of feeling or emotion. This is necessarily true of any being that is immutable, for to experience "e-motion" is literally to be "moved." The Bible often speaks of Jesus as "moved with compassion," and today we describe an occasion of deep feeling as "a profoundly moving experience." In the classical view feelings were a flaw, emotions a defect that diverted persons from a more rational course. In Stoicism the ethical ideal was to control life by reason, unswayed by emotion. So the ideal person was one who had learned not to feel, who had cultivated *apatheia.* Similarly, the perfect being is the apathetic being, unencumbered by the feelings and emotions that agitate us lesser beings. God, then, is by definition both immutable and impassible.

The word *pathos,* from which "apathy" and "impassibility" are derived, also means "suffering." The "passion" narrative, for instance, is the story of Christ's suffering. To suffer is to be affected (that is, moved) by something outside oneself, which is inconsistent with the Greek notion of immutability. So an impassible God is a God that cannot suffer.

Theologically this created some problems for early Christianity, because Jesus, the incarnate second person of the Trinity, is confessed to have "suffered under Pontius Pilate." If God by definition cannot suffer, then God the Son could not have suffered under Pontius Pilate. One solution was to say that even though God the Son suffered, God the Father did not. Such a split personality within the Godhead contradicted orthodox theology, however, for the doctrine of *perichoresis* (coinherence) asserted that each person of the Trinity participates fully in the being of the others. The fall-back position was to claim that while the human Jesus suffered, the divine Son did not, but a schizoid Christ was equally inconsistent with orthodoxy, for much the same reason. Still another proposed solution was to claim that the divine Christ didn't really suffer, but only appeared to suffer. This was the doctrine of Docetism ("appearance"). That solution turned the passion drama into a sham, a theatrical illusion, implying that salvation in Christ was a kind of a magic trick; hence Docetism also was also rejected as a heresy.

The great Anselm, still wrestling with this dilemma in the eleventh century, tried to solve the problem this way:

> But how are You at once both merciful and impassible? For if You are impassible You do not have any compassion; and if You have no compassion Your heart is not sorrowful from compassion with the sorrowful, which is what being merciful is. But if You are not merciful whence comes so much consolation for the sorrowful?
>
> How, then, are You merciful and not merciful, O Lord, unless it be that You are merciful in relation to us and not in relation to Yourself? In fact, You are [merciful] according to our way of looking at things and not according to Your way. For when You look upon us in our misery it is we who feel the effect of Your mercy, but You do not experience the feeling. Therefore You are both merciful because You save the sorrowful and pardon sinners against You; and You are not merciful because You do not experience any feeling of compassion for misery.[3]

What a marvel of equivocation, illustrating the impossibility of reconciling impassibility with the biblical view of divine compassion. What can "steadfast love" be for an apathetic God? Because the God of classical theism cannot actually be affected by us creatures and by the things that happen to us in the world, "love" can at most describe a one-way relationship from Creator to creatures. God's love can only be giving, not receiving or reciprocal. What the divine love must mean, then, is that the omniscient God has foreseen and provided for all our needs in advance. No notion of God's love as relational or empathic is even thinkable on this theological turf.

Contemporary Revisions

The classical conception of God dominated Western theology
for eighteen centuries, although it never fully captured public
worship, which retained its focus on the suffering Son of God,
or private spirituality, which continued to use emotive images
to express the divine-human relationship. In the twentieth century, however, this classical view of divine perfection has become so remote from human experience and the contemporary
worldview that the very concept of God has undergone a quiet
revolution.

People today place high value on relationships, on deep and
honest feelings, and on personal growth and development. It is
often said that the process is more important than the product.
There are parallels to this in the changing understanding of the
natural world. According to the theory of relativity, everything is
related to everything else and affected by everything else. Drop
a pebble in the water, and eventually the ripples will reach the
farthest shore. The universe is like that. Also everything is an
incessant dance of energy, in perpetual flux: $E = mc^2$. The two
modern concepts come together in the model of a universe of
dynamic relations.

These changing perceptions of what is real and what is valuable have had a profound effect on theological thinking over the
past century, even though the change has been so gradual that
many have not noticed it. As our guides in exploring the implications for theology of this new way of perceiving the world, I
have chosen three prominent thinkers: Alfred North Whitehead,
Abraham Joshua Heschel, and Jürgen Moltmann.

Alfred North Whitehead

Whitehead was the great turn-of-the-century mathematician who
collaborated with Bertrand Russell in producing the monumen-
tal *Principia Mathematica,* which, half a century later, became
the foundation for the so-called "new math." He was a man of
exceeding breadth. From mathematics he branched out into the
philosophy of science, and he also savored the romantic poets,
especially Wordsworth. Long before C. P. Snow, he dreamed of
bringing the "two cultures" together in a single, embracing truth.
As a young man he purchased a large collection of theological

works, but after a few months he had read enough and called his bookseller to cart them away. Later in life, when he constructed his magnum opus, *Process and Reality: An Essay in Cosmology,* he returned to that earlier interest, for God had become the keystone in the arch of his cosmology.[4]

As the title of *Process and Reality* suggests, Whitehead saw reality as continuously in flux. It is a mistake to think, with Newton, that there are permanent things that are always in motion. Rather, basic reality is motion, a ceaseless dance of energy. The features of the world that appear more stable and permanent are but abstractions from the dynamic concreteness of reality. If "dynamic concreteness" sounds like a contradiction in terms, that's because we've lost the etymological root of "concrete," as in "con-crescence," which literally means, "growing together."

That's what life is, in Whitehead's view: a succession of moments, in each of which many influences grow together to form a single, concrete moment of actuality. Whitehead's model for this is our own subjective awareness. That has sometimes been pictured as a "stream of consciousness," but the image of a stream does not do justice to the episodic nature of life. Our waking hours are filled by one decision after another, each responding to relevant factors and moving to closure by cutting off alternative possibilities. For instance, I get up in the morning, look over the available shirts to wear, and, taking into consideration the events of the upcoming day, choose one to put on. Then I turn to the next decision — probably which tie to wear with the chosen shirt. If the larger events of our daily lives have this episodic character, it is reasonable to assume that the briefest intervals of experience are also episodic, even though such brief instants are scarcely observable.

In Whitehead's scheme, all reality consists of many such moments, occurring both simultaneously and in succession. Cosmic process is a chain of events, with each moment of growing-together in turn becoming one of the influences on future moments of growing-together, in endless, pulsating sequence. Process, development, growth, maturation, individuation — these are the fundamental notions in Whitehead's view. It's a biological model of reality, or perhaps even more, a psychological model, with significant social and historical dimensions as well.

Whitehead finds problematic those purely mathematical descriptions of the natural world that one often finds in the natural sciences. Such descriptions may be accurate as far as they go, but they are objective and external and cannot get at what existence really is from the inside. Mathematical descriptions are thus abstractions from the whole. To regard them as the entire reality is to commit "the fallacy of misplaced concreteness," Whitehead insists. The only reality we know from the inside is, of course, ourselves, and that subjective reality is not only a series of decisions, as we have noted, but a bundle of feelings, in myriad colors and flavors. What would human existence be if we took away all feeling? Whatever might remain would certainly not be recognizable as *human,* for human experience is constituted of feeling. Furthermore, we encounter the external world through our senses, and we come to know other persons through empathy, which means "feeling-in" to what another is feeling.[5]

At this point Whitehead puts Wordsworth's poetry together with quantum physics and hypothesizes that reality is rhythmic, pulsating feeling, a continuous sequence of droplets of energy in an endless chain of sympathetic response. Each pulse or droplet or quantum of feeling constitutes a single, momentary occasion of experience, commencing with the feeling of all the influences in the relevant world, and integrating those diverse feelings into an instant of completion, which, in turn, projects itself into the future as an influence on succeeding moments of experience. Whitehead's philosophy of organism is an atomic theory, with each atom being one of these moments of experience. Whitehead calls each moment of feeling or occasion of experience an "actual entity," because such a moment of feeling is what is ultimately real, the building-block out of which everything else is made.

Whitehead was impressed by the creativity in the world process, constantly generating novelty as the universe develops. He therefore theorized that each actual entity or moment of experience is endowed with a certain degree of freedom, however limited, to shape its own integration or "satisfaction." Once that satisfaction is achieved, it is then thrust into the future as an influence on succeeding occasions. This means that the future cannot be known with much precision, not even by God, because the future is yet to be determined by the decisions of the countless actual entities that make up the world at any given time.

In Whitehead's metaphysics, there are no exceptions to the basic principles governing all things, so what is true of other actualities also applies to God. God knows the world in the same way that other beings know their environing world: by sympathetic involvement in it. The divine difference is that God's environment is the entire universe. God not only influences all beings (as in classical theism); God is the one being who is influenced *by* all beings in the universe, and with perfect empathy. The seminary at which I teach conducts empathy training for its students. Our assumption is that all persons have some capacity to feel what others are feeling and that this capacity can be increased through training. So far, however, none of our students has achieved perfection. Even the most skilled counselors miss or misperceive nuances of feeling in other persons. God, however, is the individual who empathizes perfectly with every other actual entity across the entire range of the cosmos. Thus Whitehead's God is still "perfect being," but *perfect apathy* has been replaced by *perfect empathy.*

In this schema, each of us contributes something to God, namely, our entire experience. God empathically receives and integrates all those experiences into the divine life in God's own novel way, and they are thereby preserved everlastingly in the living memory of God. Thus God needs the world in the same way that every other actual entity needs the world: to supply the "givens" for its own experience. "Each temporal occasion embodies God and is embodied in God," says Whitehead.[6]

God receives from the world, and God also gives to the world. Because God's experience includes the entire world, past as well as present, God has the inclusive vision of what is needed by the world and each entity in it. God offers to each actual entity an ideal initial aim for its own fulfilment. If the God-given aim were actualized by each and every actual entity, then God's will would be done, on earth as it is in heaven. As we noted, however, each actual entity has its own modicum of freedom, and it may therefore choose not to actualize the God-given aim, or to actualize it only partially. The concept of moral evil is here universalized to all actual entities, for the possibility of rejecting or distorting God's aim is the opening for evil to enter the world.

God acts on the world by persuasion, by the alluring power
of an ideal vision, and that is the only power God exerts in the
world in Whitehead's system. This ideal held before us is the
divine "lure." Theologian Bernard Lee speaks of God "beckon-
ing" us into an ideal future.[7] The notion is also well-captured
in Robert F. Kennedy's favorite quotation, "Some see things as
they are and ask, 'why?'; I dream things that never were and
ask, 'why not?'"

This allure of the divine vision is, of course, mostly subconscious. It burrows into our imagination and breaks forth in our
dreams and visions. Occasionally there are outcroppings into
public consciousness. One such is the vision of God's Reign set
before us by the man from Galilee.

Whitehead's metaphysics is complex and filled with technical
terms, but this brief survey may be adequate to show the import
of his thought for our understanding of God. The perfection of
Whitehead's God is not only a perfect giving (the initial aim) but
also a perfect receiving, an unfailing empathy for all beings —
the very opposite of the classical doctrine of impassibility. Obviously such a God cares very deeply about creatures, all of whom
contribute their own substance to the divine life. As a consequence, God suffers with us, a truth which Whitehead finds best
expressed on Golgotha. "God," he concludes at the end of *Process and Reality,* "is the great companion — the fellow-sufferer
who understands."[8] This God, unlike that of classical theism, is
deeply involved in the world, but God's power in the world is
solely the influence of the divine love, exercised afresh in each
and every moment. God respects the freedom of each entity
to determine its own course, and that means that at any given
place and time, the divine will may be thwarted. God receives
perfectly as well as gives perfectly. We offer ourselves, "our souls
and bodies as a living sacrifice," to quote the liturgy. And, in
contrast to the classical God who cannot receive anything, God
receives our gifts into the divine life, where they are treasured
eternally.

Abraham Heschel

While Whitehead attacked the doctrine of the apathetic God
philosophically, Abraham Heschel criticized it from a biblical
perspective. Author, Hasidic mystic, and refugee from the Nazis,

Heschel found his way to the U.S. in 1940, where he achieved renown as a teacher, writer, and leader in the civil rights and anti-war movements. In 1962 he published *The Prophets,* dedicated to the victims of the Holocaust.[9]

The typical scholar's way to approach the prophets is to ask, "What is their idea of God?" That is the wrong question, says Heschel, for the prophets did not develop a new concept or theory about God. What the prophets had was a personal knowledge of God that can come only from intimate acquaintance. The prophetic word emerges out of the prophet's emotional life with God. Says Heschel:

> Prophetic sympathy is a response to transcendent sensibility. It is . . . the assimilation of the prophet's emotional life to the divine. . . . The emotional experience of the prophet becomes the focal point for the prophet's understanding of God. He lives not only his personal life, but also the life of God. The prophet hears God's voice and feels [God's] heart. . . . As an imparter his soul overflows, speaking as he does out of the fullness of his sympathy.[10]

The prophet's sympathy with the divine heart is *"a sympathy with the divine pathos."*[11] Heschel has chosen his words carefully. His primary thesis is that in the prophets we discover God's pathos through the prophets' sympathetic response to that pathos.

What does Heschel mean by "the pathos of God"? Certainly he includes compassion, mercy, justice, steadfast love. Most fundamentally, however, he means God's intimate relatedness to humankind, God's involvement in human history. Heschel insists that pathos is more a theological category than a psychological one, because pathos includes ethos and logos, that is, intention and reason. Divine wrath, for instance, is not a matter of God getting carried away in an emotional fit of temper. Rather, anger is an expression of the intensity of God's concern.[12] Pathos, then,

> is not a passion, an unreasoned emotion, but an act formed with intention, rooted in decision and determination; not an attitude taken arbitrarily, but one charged with ethos. . . . Its essential meaning is not to be seen in its psychological

denotation, as standing for a state of the soul, but in its
theological connotation, signifying God as involved in history, as intimately affected by events in history, as living
care.[13]

The fact that the actions of humans affect not only their own
lives, but also the life of God, means that humankind is "a factor in the life of God."[14] The prophets "not only sense God in
history, but also *history in God*,"[15] a statement also made by
Whitehead and Moltmann. Such a claim would be impossible
in the classical tradition, for the classical God is unaffected by
humans and their history.

We can illustrate the pathos of God with a few brief passages from the prophets. The book of the prophet Isaiah opens
with God's sorrow because of the rebellion of Israel, expressed
through the metaphor of abandonment by one's children:

> Hear, O heavens, and give ear, O earth;
> For the Lord has spoken:
> Sons have I reared and brought up,
> But they have rebelled against Me.
> The ox knows its owner
> And the ass its master's crib;
> But Israel does not know,
> My people does not understand. (Isa. 1:2–3)[16]

Here God's pathos is the anguish of an estranged parent. These
are scarcely the words of a self-detached ruler, Heschel observes.

In a comparable passage, Hosea expresses God's conflicted
feelings of anger and compassion toward the people of God, an
emotional contradiction in which compassion must finally win
out.

> How shall I give you up, O Ephraim!
> How shall I surrender you, O Israel?
> How can I make you like Admah!
> How can I treat you like Zeboiim!
> My heart is turned within Me,
> My compassion grows like a flame.
> I will not execute My fierce anger,
> I will not again destroy Ephraim;

> For I am God and not man,
> The Holy One in your midst,
> And I will not come to destroy. (Hos. 11:8–9)[17]

Note that God's holiness does not here mean that God is above it all, unsullied by the world, but in the thick of things: "I am the Holy One in your midst."

In Jeremiah, when calamity finally strikes Jerusalem, God calls for a time of mourning:

> Thus says the Lord of hosts:
> Consider, and call for the mourning women to come;
> Let them make haste and raise a wailing over *us,*
> That our eyes may run down with tears,
> And our eyelids gush with water. (Jer. 9:17–18)[18]

Heschel calls our attention to the verse in which the Lord calls on the people to "raise a wailing over *us.*" With Israel's distress, God, too, is afflicted, and God joins the people in their grieving.

Thus Heschel finds in the prophets a very different picture from the detached and apathetic God of the classical tradition, Jewish and Christian alike. Here God is deeply engaged with the people, involved in their history, frustrated by their evil choices, angry over their desertion, yet compassionately committed to a future together with God's people.

Jürgen Moltmann

Jürgen Moltmann builds on the foundations laid by Whitehead and Heschel, both of whom he cites in his writings. During World War II Moltmann, still in his teens, served in the *Wehrmacht.* Afterwards he was a prisoner of war in Great Britain for three years. Those years behind barbed wire gave him a deep sense of solidarity with prisoners, refugees, and oppressed people everywhere. Upon his release, Moltmann returned to a country responsible for the Holocaust. As a theologian, he puzzled over the relationship of God to all this suffering that had affected him so profoundly. He became convinced that the only theology worth its salt was a theology that could address the issue of the enormous weight of human affliction. He was an early admirer of Dietrich Bonhoeffer, whose prison aphorism,

"Only a suffering God can help," impressed itself deeply on his mind. His concern to hold theology and suffering close together is well illustrated in his reaction to a letter received from an Argentinian friend at Christmastime in 1978. The letter begins, "Is it possible to celebrate life in the midst of death?" The writer then describes the repressive violence in Argentina, the unemployment, the deepening poverty, the rising rate of infant mortality. In response Moltmann asks,

> Is it possible honestly to celebrate the victory of Christ, or to see life as a festival, in a world like this? For so many people, victory seems to be swallowed up in death, and hell seems triumphant.[19]

For Moltmann it is Christ and his cross that provide the point of contact between suffering humanity and God. Jesus came preaching that the Reign of God had drawn nigh to the poor, the lost, and the marginated: "He entered into the way of suffering."[20] The world's afflicted and persecuted people can identify with Jesus, because he has identified with them. He is "Christ our brother, who is our companion on the path through fear, temptation, imprisonment, exile and abandonment by God himself."[21]

This identification of Jesus with suffering and abandoned humanity comes to a climax in the passion story, especially in Jesus' cry of dereliction from the cross, "My God, my God, why hast thou forsaken me?" (Mark 15:34).

How could it be that Jesus' God, so intimately present as to be called "Abba" ("Daddy"), had now left his son in the lurch? How could it be that the One whose dawning Reign Jesus had proclaimed had left the herald of that Reign hanging on a cross? Why? This is the cry of every suffering person, and every suffering person can identify with Jesus' anguish. Moltmann quotes Luther's forceful expression of Jesus' predicament:

> Not only in the eyes of the world and his disciples, nay, even in his own eyes did Christ see himself as lost, as forsaken by God, felt in his conscience that he was cursed by God — suffered the torment of the damned who feel God's eternal wrath, shrink back from it and flee.[22]

Moltmann notes that the early critics of Christianity compared the dying words of Jesus unfavorably with the more heroic final words of Socrates. Apparently two of the four gospel writers also were embarrassed by the cry of desolation reported in Mark, for they substitute more fitting last words. In place of Jesus' cry of abandonment taken from Psalm 22:1, Luke uses Psalm 31:6, "Into thy hands I commit my spirit!" (Luke 23:46), while the Fourth Gospel has simply, "It is finished" (John 19:30). In corroboration of the Markan version, Moltmann cites Hebrews 2:9, "Far from God he tasted death for us all," and 5:7, "Jesus offered up prayers and supplications, with loud cries and tears."[23] Moltmann concludes, "The history of the tradition being as it is, it can be accepted that the difficult reading of Mark is as close as may be to historical reality."[24]

Across the centuries more theological ink has been expended trying to explain Jesus' cry of dereliction than almost any other text in the New Testament. "What theology *can* endure in the face of Jesus' dying cry?" Moltmann asks.[25] He found a turning-point when he changed the question from "What does the cross mean for us?" to "What does the cross mean for God?"[26] He elaborates:

> Is God so absolute and sovereign that he reigns in heavenly glory, incapable of suffering and untouched by the death of his Son? And if God is essentially incapable of suffering, does this not mean that he is incapable of love as well? But if he is incapable of love, he is poorer than any man or woman who is able to love and suffer.[27]

To make sense out of the passion narrative, Moltmann realized, one must presuppose not the apathetic God of classical antiquity, but the *pathos* of God enunciated by the prophets. Recalling Paul's affirmation that "God was in Christ, reconciling the world to himself" (2 Cor. 5:19), Moltmann began to take more seriously "the presence of God in Jesus' suffering and death" and "the presence of Jesus' suffering and death in God."[28] We will understand Moltmann only if we recognize that his thinking here is fully incarnational and trinitarian, so that the cross is *in God* as well as on Calvary, and what happens takes place first of all between God the Father and God the Son. God cries out to God, and God is abandoned by God. "In the cross of

Christ," he writes, "a rupture tears, as it were, through God himself."[29] It is a moment of suffering for the Father as well as for the Son, an act of surrendering love in which the Father gives up his Son and the Son gives up himself, so that God may be fully immersed in the suffering of the world and the suffering of the world may be fully taken up into God. Jesus' identification with suffering humanity thereby becomes *God's* identification with suffering humanity. Although Moltmann's argument is involuted, the following passage makes his meaning brilliantly clear:

> On the cross of Christ God cuts himself off from himself. He delivers himself up in order to be ours and to be with us, right into the desolation of God-forsakenness itself. Even in this hell, thou art there. That is the divine truth of Jesus' cry of desolation. And that is why, on the other hand, we cannot shut out any suffering or any loss or any grief from God. If we discover God in forsakenness and desolation, and if every forsakenness we have to endure is taken up in God, then we even win back the elements of truth in pantheism. "In him we live and move and have our being." Nothing is shut off from God, if God himself has gone through the experience of Christ's cross.[30]

From that event in the life of God, the trinitarian movement is completed, as the Spirit flows forth into the world, the Spirit "which upholds the abandoned, justifies the despised, and will bring the dead to life."[31]

In Wiesel's autobiographical novel *Night,* Moltmann finds an episode that becomes for him a modern parable communicating the meaning of the cross. It is a story that draws on the Jewish tradition of the *shekinah,* that is, God's indwelling presence with God's people in the midst of their affliction:

> The SS hanged two Jewish men and a youth in front of the whole camp. The men died quickly, but the death throes of the youth lasted for half an hour. "Where is God? Where is he?" someone asked behind me. As the youth still hung in torment in the noose after a long time, I heard the man call again, "Where is God now?" And I heard a voice in

myself answer: "Where is he? He is here. He is hanging [here] on the gallows.... "[32]

"Any other answer would be blasphemy," Moltmann comments. "To speak here of a God who could not suffer would make God a demon."[33]

Thus the good news of the cross in Moltmann's gospel is that there is no affliction that God through Christ has not shared with us, including even the experience of God-forsakenness itself. "There is no loneliness and no rejection which he has not taken to himself and assumed in the cross of Jesus."[34]

Moltmann identifies two earlier thinkers who share this theological vision: Spanish Catholic Miguel de Unamuno ("God suffers in each and all of us,... and we all suffer in him"[35]), and Russian Orthodox Nicholas Berdyaev ("The fate of the crucified Son of God... is nothing other than the tragic mystery of suffering which the Godhead himself endures"[36]). Yet Moltmann can agree only partially, for were this suffering of God the total gospel, the Good News would be nothing more than a tragedy — for God as well as for us. There would be no liberation from suffering and no triumph over evil. Suffering, in fact, would be "given an eternal permanence."[37] That amounts to a truncated gospel, Calvary without Easter:

> We must not linger in Gethsemane and beneath the cross endlessly repeating what it teaches us of pain and fear. Without the resurrection, the cross really is quite simply a tragedy and nothing more than that.... This path from the cross to the resurrection is Christ's passover, the new exodus into eternal liberty.[38]

Moltmann, better known for his theology of hope than for his theology of the cross, always holds the two together: crucifixion and resurrection, Good Friday and Easter, suffering and hope. Furthermore, resurrection itself is "not merely a consolation in suffering," but a sign of *"God's great protest"* against suffering and death.[39] The resurrection is God's demonstration that what now is, is not what is meant to be. Hence faith in the risen Christ does not make persons content to accept life as it is, but impatient to transform the present world in the direction of the

Reign that is coming. "Instead of being reconciled to existing reality they begin to suffer from it and to resist it."[40]

> Faith...shares in God's protest, by rising up out of the apathy of misery (and even more out of the cynicism of prosperity) and by fighting against death in the midst of life. Death is the evil power already existing in life's midst, not just at its end. Here is the economic death of the starving, there the political death of the oppressed. Here is the social death of the handicapped; there the noisy death through bombs; and here again the silent death of petrified souls. The raising of Christ is proved by our courage to rise against death....We show our hope for the life that defeats death in our protest against the manifold forms of death in the midst of life. It is only in the passion for life and our giving of ourselves for its liberation that we entrust ourselves utterly to the God who raises the dead.[41]

Thus in much the same way that Whitehead's divine "lure" draws us toward the divine vision, the dawning Reign of God casts its light into the present, so that eternal hope kindles daily hope. Passion, hope, and liberation are thus held together in Moltmann's message.

God and the Lone Ranger

When I was a boy, my father used to travel a great deal. He would often be away for a week or more at a stretch. The picture of his returning is indelibly etched in my mind. I would be standing in the foyer, waiting for him to come in the door. I was overjoyed to see him, yet I would clasp my hands tightly behind me and bite my lips to keep from showing the feelings that were welling up in me. As a boy of five, I had somewhere gotten the message that real men don't show feelings.

My favorite radio hero in those days before television was the Lone Ranger. He was a man of action who could ride into a situation that no one in town could handle, and in thirty minutes he would solve the problem single-handed. Repeatedly he would demonstrate his amazing control by using just the right amount of force. He never got angry, and he never killed anyone. Usually he just shot the gun out of the bad guy's hand. At the end people would try to thank him, but he would be riding off on his great horse, Silver, before any such outpouring of emotion could embarrass him. Somewhere in the picture was his tagalong buddy, Tonto, but the Lone Ranger didn't seem to really *need* him. Occasionally the two would discuss strategy together, Tonto using broken English, but never did the Lone Ranger share a moment of genuine intimacy or real vulnerability. I can't picture him weeping. He was the very model of self-control and self-sufficiency. He had it all together. He was my ideal. He was the perfect exemplar of the Stoic "apathetic man." All this penetrated deep into my psyche, and in many ways it is still operative there.

Happily, values have been changing for my sons, even though the Lone Ranger lingers on. They have grown up in an age that values feelings and their honest expression. Spock of "Star Trek," that space-age representative of the apathetic man, is more pitied than admired for his lack of emotion. Robert Bellah observes that today "the 'interpersonal' seems to be the key to much of life."[42] Intimacy is treasured, and it is no longer considered a euphemism for sex. But intimacy involves risk, vulnerability, and empathy. When we can acknowledge our genuine vulnerability, then we find freedom in relationships rather than in self-sufficiency. Action is still valued, but we have also learned the importance of attending to the concerns of others before taking action. Listening, consulting, and counseling skills are prized. Even business today focuses on cooperative problem-solving. The "Lone Ranger" who rides in with a ready-made solution is regarded as a bull in the china shop. Increasingly the leader most admired is the one who knows how to empower others instead of wielding personal power.

All this has had a profound impact on the way we understand and relate to God. As old as Genesis is the recognition that our notions of human and divine reflect each other. To be sure, we must beware of simply making God in our image:

> For my thoughts are not your thoughts,
> neither are your ways my ways,
> says the Lord.
> For as the heavens are higher than the earth,
> so are my ways higher than your ways
> and my thoughts than your thoughts. (Isa. 55:8–9)

We cannot avoid imaging God in some way, but however that may be done, "the greatest conceivable" cannot be less than human: "My ways are higher than your ways." Beyond that, we need to allow our ideas of true greatness to be shaped by the scriptures, and especially by the reflection of God in the face of Jesus Christ.

Biblical studies and contemporary experience are converging on a new concept of God that represents a radical change from the tradition in significant respects, notably its ideas of divine relatedness and divine power. Where classical antiquity's ideal of the apathetic human found its counterpart in the apathetic God, today's valuing of vulnerability, empathy, and honest feeling are mirrored in the theology of the suffering God. "The most important progress in Christian theology today is being made in overcoming the 'apathy' axiom in theology," Moltmann asserts.[43] This is not a rejection of the idea of divine perfection as such, but a rethinking of what true greatness really is. Moltmann approvingly quotes Robert Browning, who in this regard was a century ahead of the theologians:

> For the loving worm within its clod,
> Were diviner than a loveless God
> Amid his worlds, I would dare to say.[44]

Today we are recovering the God of pathos of the prophets and the passionate God of the cross, the One who weeps with those who weep and rejoices with those who rejoice, the high priest who is able to sympathize with our weakness (Heb. 4:15). This biblical God who is re-emerging into our awareness is not a distant God, living somewhere in the far reaches of Kafka's Castle, but the intimate God of the prophets and the "Abba" of Jesus' prayer. It is a two-way relationship, in which God not only influences us but is influenced by us, by our prayers and our deeds. God's love is steadfast, and in respect to its steadfastness, it is indeed unchanging. Yet no one loves another without becoming vulnerable to the other, without being affected by the other, and, if need be, suffering with the other; hence one who loves, especially with a steadfast love, will necessarily be changed in the loving relationship. In this regard it is notable that in Hosea even God's holiness, which is so often regarded as God's unsullied otherness, is holiness "in your midst." The fact that God is in some respects changeless and in other respects changing is not really a paradox. Anyone who has experienced constant love understands this.

The nature of divine power is also being reconsidered in twentieth-century theology. In the doctrinal tradition that took shape in the Roman Empire, says Moltmann, God was thought of "as an all-powerful, perfect and infinite being, ... understood in terms of the image of the Egyptian pharaohs, the Persian kings and the Roman emperors."[45] Such worship of God as naked power too easily becomes oppressive and even sadistic and can be used to endorse political tyranny.[46] Furthermore, that picture of God is inconsistent with vast stretches of scripture. Heschel states, "The idea of divine omnipotence, holding God responsible for everything, expecting Him to do the impossible, to defy human freedom, is a non-Jewish idea."[47] The God of the scriptures is less concerned to demonstrate divine power than to liberate and empower God's children. The Son of God comes among God's people as a suffering servant and teaches that "whoever would be great among you must be your servant" (Matt. 20:26), a verse used in the Barmen Declaration to oppose the Führer-principle.[48] Yet even so, "the weakness of God is stronger than men" (1 Cor. 1:25).

From the confluence of the theologies of process, hope, and liberation, the concept of divine power that is emerging is one of persuasive love rather than coercive force, ruling through the alluring vision of the Reign of God. Far from giving all power to God at the expense of humans, who are thereby rendered powerless,[49] these theologies envision a God whose strength is in liberating empowerment, not in overpowering force. This is a God who, though not omnipotent in the popular sense, is "all-sufficient" (to use Fackre's term) — able to accomplish divine purposes through means that are consistent with the divine being.

There are those who, having heard all this, will still say, "Give me the God who can act decisively to heal my illness, to solve my problem, to make it right." By comparison, the compassionate Companion sounds weak — "pathetic," in fact. Still, there is power in that weakness. A pastor of my acquaintance did a year's internship as a chaplain at the Hershey Medical Center. He reported that it is common for patients suddenly confronted by a threatening illness to feel that God is ab-

sent, or even that God has abandoned them. Moltmann himself
says,

> Anyone who suffers without cause first thinks that he has
> been forsaken by God. God seems to him to be the mys-
> terious, incomprehensible God who destroys the good for-
> tune that he gave.[50]

For such persons prayer seems to be swallowed up in silence,
if prayer is possible at all. That reaction almost seems to be a
reflex response to bad news; yet I wonder how much people are
conditioned to make such a response by the notion of God as the
all-controlling manager of human affairs, who can make everything right with a flick of the divine finger. Then, when things
don't quickly turn out right, they feel betrayed or abandoned by
God. A chaplain at a hospital sponsored by a prominent faith
healer told me that too many of their patients are "set up" for
just such a reaction. When no divine "quick fix" is forthcoming,
their affliction is compounded by the feeling of abandonment by
the One who surrounds life and death with meaning. How much
sounder the God of Jeremiah who joins us in our anguish and
grief, or the God of the cross who is present even within our
very cry of abandonment.

Does this amount to an endorsement of suffering, to divine
resignation in the face of evil? Not at all, for the resurrection
and the promise of God's coming Reign are, in Moltmann's
words, "God's great protest." The vision of a world in which
God reigns has always led God's people to be impatient with
things as they are and to strain forward to that which is coming.
Exactly how that will come about we cannot say, and specula-
tion about the time and mode wastes spiritual energy that might
better be expended living in accordance with God's Reign. We
do know that God's Reign will not come into being because *we*
build it. That was the fallacy of an earlier theological liberalism.
At the end of the twentieth century we know that humankind
is too deeply infected by evil to be able to accomplish that. Yet
perhaps it is not too much to hope that through the persuasive
power of God's Spirit, some liberating transformation of the human spirit will enable a small step forward toward the promised
Reign. That is the hope that drives the theologies of liberation
and keeps them from despairing in the face of resistant human

evil. That is our only alternative to cynicism concerning the human prospect in the nuclear age. It is our only hope that this planet — this small piece of God's great universe — may yet escape one of the many doomsday scenarios forecast by the experts in futuring. And so we pray, "Thy kingdom come, thy will be done, on earth as it is in heaven."

Chapter 6

We Shall Overcome: Human Communion in Affliction and Joy

I recall a Maryknoll sister whom I met in at the First International Congress on Suffering at Notre Dame in 1979. In our discussion group her words and demeanor communicated a quiet confidence in God's presence and God's love. She listened patiently as others agonized over the "why" question and debated the nature of evil. She herself expended little energy trying to solve such mysteries. For her the urgent issue was how to embody Christ's compassion for the world's afflicted and combat the evils causing that affliction.

It is to this more practical question that we turn in this chapter. What are the resources of the community of faith for helping people to cope with suffering and resist the powers of evil? The question will be addressed under four headings. We will begin by examining the power of personal presence with the afflicted. This will be followed by a survey of the phases of affliction and the kinds of help appropriate to each phase. Then we will consider the call to resist the powers of evil and the controversial tradition of nonviolent resistance. Finally, we will investigate the resources of the church's liturgy for coping with suffering and evil. These are not really separate topics, for personal presence is ultimately Christ's presence celebrated in the liturgy; resisting evil is the way of compassion for the oppressed; and celebrating God's presence comforts the afflicted and empowers resistance.

Presence

St. Paul compares the people of God to the human body, with each person a different organ in that body. We belong to one another as if we were all parts of a single organism. Within this community, Paul reminds us, we rejoice with those who rejoice, and weep with those who weep (Rom. 12:15; cf. 1 Cor. 12). John Donne echoed that when he wrote, "No man is an island, entire of itself; every man is a piece of the continent, a part of the main." We all belong to each other. Jesus added another dimension to that when he said, "I was hungry and you gave me food, I was thirsty and you gave me drink, I was a stranger and you welcomed me, I was naked and you clothed me, I was sick and you visited me, I was in prison and you came to me" (Matt. 25:35–36). Not only do we all belong together, but in ministering to one another, we are also ministering to Christ. Luther reversed the image in calling upon the faithful to be "Christ" to their brothers and sisters. A vertical dimension is implicit in the horizontal: every human relationship also involves a relation to God. The implicit becomes explicit in Paul's metaphor, "the body of *Christ*," manifesting that God is our intimate companion in the midst of that community.

The implication of all this is the unspectacular thesis that our primary resource for coping with suffering is each other. Our presence — our personal, bodily, sacramental presence — is the most important thing we have to offer one another. A number of years ago a friend of mine whose specialty was arts in ministry suffered severe head injuries in a traffic accident. He was in critical condition when his wife, Ella (not her real name), arrived at the hospital. As she awaited word on her husband's condition, she called her pastor, who left the dinner table in order to be with her. She recalls that he stayed quite awhile, but she can't remember anything he said. She remembers his comforting touch and that he prayed with her, but most of all she remembers his being there with her.

It is important that we be there with a friend in her or his time of crisis. If it helps to bring along a pot of chicken soup, or whatever it is you usually offer, then by all means do so, but remember that the important thing is not your delicious soup, but the communication that you care, that you are available in whatever way your friend needs you. If possible, this should include your willingness to listen, without any necessity to come up with solutions. Suffering people need to talk out their hurts with someone, and it doesn't help much to talk to the walls. Sheila, introduced in chapter 2 as the one whose father died under distressing circumstances that left her questioning her faith, reported that her pastor called on her soon after the funeral. He listened empathically to her disquieting questions, but he wanted to rush her into theological answers that she wasn't prepared to accept. That's when the desire to help becomes the need to rescue. Many of us have a strong need to rescue others, perhaps because their plight is so threatening to us. We want to "rush to the resurrection," as one seminarian put it. We forget that before Easter comes Gethsemane with its question, "Could you not watch with me one hour?" A hospital chaplain was even more graphic — and equally theological: "If you want to help, you need to be willing to descend into Hell with the sufferer." For most of us, that is a terrifying prospect, yet only so can we incarnate the compassionate presence of the crucified God.

Sheila had a next-door neighbor who invited her over for coffee in the kitchen and listened to Sheila's story without laying on any agenda of her own. Sheila found that more supportive. Subsequently, when her neighbor's teen-age son was killed in an auto accident, Sheila was able to reciprocate. Henri Nouwen has this to say about such friendship:

> The friend who can be silent with us in a moment of despair or confusion, who can stay with us in an hour of grief and bereavement, who can tolerate not-knowing, not-curing, not-healing and face with us the reality of our powerlessness, that is the friend who cares.[1]

It should be encouraging to clergy as well as laity to recognize that lay persons can be effective ministers to each other, even where pastors fail.

It is not as easy to reach out and touch someone as Ma Bell would like us to believe. If there is an instinct to help, there is a counter-instinct to flee from the responsibility that entails. Donald Wilson, former pastor of First Presbyterian Church of Lancaster, Pa., observed that when he let it be known publicly that he was terminally ill, old friends would cross the street to avoid facing him. What accounts for such avoidance? Probably in part it was the subconscious awareness that facing Don Wilson meant facing one's own mortality. Closer to the surface, Wilson recognized that any traumatic change in life, whether it be terminal illness, marital break-up, loss of job, or whatever, also affects all one's relationships. Wilson's friends could not just say, "Hi, how are you?" and chat a bit, as if nothing had changed. The awful truth had to be acknowledged between them if the relationship were to continue on any meaningful level. Dealing with the dreadful reality is what leads so many of us to put off reaching out until some supposedly more opportune time. Wilson found that often he had to take the initiative and let the other know that it was all right to talk about it.

A young man recently told me that he was unable to accept his brother's terminal illness, so he avoided the topic whenever they talked. Finally his brother said, "I am dying. You have to face it. I need to talk with you about it." That word of permission from his brother opened the door to a moment of intimacy he will treasure for the rest of his life. Ministry with the afflicted usually turns out to be mutual ministry.

If we do not make the extra effort to stay in touch, the danger is that the anguish of affliction will be doubled by isolation. Sometimes the isolation comes because friends can't face the anguish, and sometimes because the hurting person cuts off support. A pastor whose wife was seriously ill let it be known that he didn't want any parishioners coming to the parsonage with their pity. The Lone Ranger rides again! One must, of course, respect the privacy of hurting people, but such a remark shouldn't be accepted at face value. I have known too many who were hurt by the added pain of isolation, even some who seemed to signal that they wanted to be left alone. After speaking at a faculty luncheon at a nearby college, I received this note from a professor who had to leave early: "You absolutely hit the nail on the head with your statement about the loneliness of suffering. How very well I know about that, having received a Ph.D. in suffering over the last twenty-two years." The basic truth is that we need each other, and even more so in time of crisis.

One reason for avoidance is that we don't know what to say. We are such speech-oriented people that we assume we need to come up with some appropriate words of comfort before we knock on the door, and we're afraid of saying the wrong thing. There are those who advise not saying anything, because a hand-squeeze or hug or kiss says all that needs to be said, but I confess to finding it difficult to visit someone without saying anything. We're going to open our mouths, and something is going to come out. We've heard the horror stories about inappropriate remarks, but know also that words can comfort.

I agree that there are indeed some bad things to say. A woman in her early twenties reported that the day after her double mastectomy, someone calling from her church told her, "You must have done something awful to deserve this!" And we have all heard the explanation given to the child who lost his daddy: "God needs him in heaven." Job's comforters clearly did their best work sitting on the dung heap with him that first week, during which "no one spoke a word to him"! (Job 2:13). If you think you need an exhaustive list of remarks to avoid, you can find it in Rabbi Kushner's book.

In truth, however, I think the fear is misplaced. Most people will appreciate the caring intent behind your fumbling words. Still, to forestall a major gaffe, here are four simple guidelines. The first is to avoid cleverness or pious platitudes. They will be recognized for what they are. The second is to be yourself. Do what comes natural to you. Third, remember that words are only a tiny fraction of communication. Ella couldn't remember what her pastor said. Finally, consider that your ears are more important than your mouth at a time like this. Not you, but the hurting person is the one who needs to talk. If you are open to listening (and not everybody is) then let that be known, and if your offer is accepted, use all the listening skills you can muster for the occasion.

Our personal presence, then — our caring and listening — is the most valuable thing we have to offer to a hurting person. With that as foundation, let us proceed to add a little more detail.

Phases of Affliction

Suffering is a process. It takes time (usually much more than people think), it requires work, and it proceeds through phases. For the person who wants to be a healing presence to another in affliction, it will be helpful to know something about the phases of suffering. Dorothee Sölle describes three phases in the suffering process, identified simply by number.[2] I find her categories illuminating, and I am much in her debt in what follows, although my phases are in some ways different from hers. Each person's suffering is unique, as Cassell already informed us in the first chapter, so it should not be surprising that no two people proceed through the phases of suffering in exactly the same way. Some may not move as quickly as others through a certain phase. Nor are there sharp boundaries between phases to indicate that a person has made the transition from one to the next. They tend to overlap, so that an individual may be working in two at the same time, or may cycle back to an earlier phase. We are, then, talking about very gross descriptions. Nevertheless, I think it is important for the helping person to identify where the sufferer is in the process of working it through.

Phase One: Impact

The first phase is the "impact" phase. A person who has undergone the kind of threat to personal intactness that we examined in the first chapter has received a tremendous emotional shock. A person's psychological world is shattered, and along with it the sense that this is a benign, comprehensible, and meaningful world. The normal immediate reaction to that, says Dr. Mardi Horowitz, is "an outcry of fear, rage or sadness at the terrible impact on one's life."[3] Horowitz himself titles this first phase "outcry." It is a time of great emotional turmoil, and the strong feelings that dominate this phase must find release. An individual who has just lost someone close, through death or divorce or other means, needs to express that grief. One who has been fired from her job or felt the sting of discrimination will have to deal with the anger she feels about that. In fact, almost any form of affliction leaves one feeling powerless, and anger is the emotional reflex to powerlessness. If those feelings remain bottled up inside, they can inflict tremendous psychological and even physical damage, until they finally find expression.

Let me illustrate what I mean by the intensity of feeling. In a teaching hospital that has a program of Clinical Pastoral Education, a young seminarian was just beginning his first visit to his assigned floor, wearing his brand new chaplain's badge. A man in a white coat scurrying down the hall stopped long enough to tell him that someone in room 318 needed to see a minister right away. So the novice chaplain eagerly entered 318 and introduced himself to the patient. "You're a chaplain?" the patient shouted. "You're a man of God? Who asked you to come in here? Get out! I don't want to see you now, I don't want to see you ever!"

The crestfallen would-be chaplain quickly withdrew and dashed back to the pastoral care office, ready to quit the program and demit the ministry, even though he wasn't sure just why he had failed so miserably. His supervisor, however, wouldn't allow him to quit and insisted that he return to the scene. So the next morning the young chaplain gingerly re-entered room 318. Much to his surprise, the patient greeted him warmly, apologized for his outburst, and explained what had taken place the previous day. Just before the chaplain had come into the room, his surgeon had informed him that his condition was terminal, and that he had only a few months to live, after which the surgeon had promptly retreated from the room. The chaplain had become the target of convenience for the patient's anger at the news he had received and its mode of communication.

It is not always that easy to vent the strong feelings that well up following the initial shock. Sometimes those emotions are so overpowering that we have to suppress them temporarily in order to get on with what needs to be done. At the time of my father's death I can remember *not* feeling. It was almost a feeling of not feeling. This is numbing, or denial. It's a kind of natural anaesthetic that stretches those powerful emotions out over time to keep us from being overwhelmed, so that we can deal with the shattered world at a more manageable pace. Horowitz notes that for weeks or months after a disaster, there can be oscillation back and forth between denial and intrusive thoughts of the traumatic event, as one slowly allows the awful reality to seep into one's awareness.[4]

Another reason why we find it hard to express our pain is that we have difficulty finding language adequate to voice the depth of what's happening to us, probably unlike anything we've been through before. In fact, the suffering person is sure that nobody can possibly understand, because nobody's been through anything like this before. Strictly speaking, that's true, which is why the remark, "I know just what you're going through," is sure to be rejected. *Nobody* else knows just what *this* person is going through. That makes expression of feeling all the harder and the temptation to isolate oneself greater. "The pressure of suffering turns one in on himself," says Sölle in describing this phase.[5] Elie Wiesel states that it was ten years before he was able to write about his experience in the death camps, because it was so hard to find language adequate to express what he had experienced. Thus the impact phase oscillates between muteness and outcry. Blessed is the one who can help another give voice to the inexpressible!

Another common feature of phase one is that the individual's world narrows to the specific event in which he or she is engrossed. A person with a terrible toothache cannot attend to anything else. Wiesel tells how hunger turned him into all stomach. "Bread, soup — these were my whole life," he writes. "I was a body. Perhaps less than that even: a starved stomach."[6]

When the suffering person finally breaks through the language barrier, the story will come pouring out, as deep emotions suddenly find form in narrative. The story gets told over and over. It seems that one can't tell it often enough, until friends, pastor, counselor, all get tired of hearing it. When I was in Mobile, Ala., six months after Hurricane Frederick hit that city with incredible force, I found people eager to tell me what had happened to them during the hurricane, even that long after the event. One of them explained, "We've gotten tired of listening to each other, so it's great when an outsider comes in."

So immersed in their own stories can persons become that they often see their stories in places that seem totally unrelated. Several years ago a student in one of my courses was just beginning to work through a painful divorce. One of the assigned texts was Wiesel's *Night*. I was puzzled when she told me that she loved the book because she found herself on every page. I wondered how it could be that this woman, too young to have experienced the war, would find herself in a story about life in concentration camps. Soon it became apparent that the oppression, abuse, and general hell of the camp symbolized what her marriage had been for her.

These, then, are the characteristics I find in the impact phase of the suffering process: deep feeling, often dampened by numbing; alternation between muteness and outcry; powerlessness; isolation; immersion in the suffering event; the need to tell the story and do so repeatedly.

Phase Two: Working Through

The second phase I call "working through," a term borrowed from Horowitz, who describes it as "facing the reality of what has happened."[7] Here the suffering person begins to put life back together, and this requires rational processes that were not possible when he or she was still reeling under the impact. Much of this "working through" will be very practical decision-making regarding such things as child custody, selling the house, changing jobs. The helper who attempts problem-solving with a person in the emotional throes of phase one is likely to find that the process is going in circles, and that poor decisions are being made. Feelings continue strong into phase two, but now the sufferer can move beyond mere survival and start putting things in order financially, legally, and socially. He or she begins to feel more in control of life, less buffeted by the slings and arrows of outrageous fortune, less overwhelmed by uncontrollable feelings. Communication improves also, as one begins to feel less isolated, less need to be immersed in one's private world of pain, less obsession with one's own story, and greater ability to articulate for another what one is feeling and thinking. With less need for denial, the person can begin to accept the situation, or at least become resigned to it. So the transition from the first to the second phase is a movement from feeling toward thinking, from denial toward acceptance, from powerlessness toward control within the situation, from isolation to communication. A supportive community can help a person move through this phase by offering very practical skills as well as continuing emotional support and genuine friendship.

This is a more rational phase in another sense also. In chapter 1 we noted that by its very nature, suffering throws into question the meaning of one's life. Psychologist Ronnie Janoff-Bulman states, "Whenever someone becomes victimized by a disaster, whatever its nature, their most basic assumptions about themselves and the world are undermined. Psychological recovery, to a large extent, requires rebuilding those assumptions."[8] So part of the aftermath will be trying to reconcile the traumatic event with one's religious faith. The anguished question "Why?" takes on a different meaning in this phase than it had in the feeling phase. Every pastor has had the experience of being confronted with the "why" question in the initial phase of a crisis of suffering. "Why is this happening to me, pastor? Why is God doing this to me?" In the impact phase, the question is not a request for a theological explanation but an emotional outburst, and no religious rationale will satisfy. The question is really an angry protest, and the skilled listener will hear and respond to the deep feeling being expressed. Months later the same question, voiced in a different emotional tone, may well be an invitation to share in the struggle to renew faith. If, in this situation, the helping friend responds by saying, "You're really angry at God, aren't you? Let's talk about what you're feeling," he or she may have missed the point in the opposite direction.

Although each person will respond differently to personal tragedy, each must find some way to redeem the significance of what has happened. Joni Eareckson, the quadraplegic who published her autobiography under the title *Joni,* decided that God had caused her accident in order that she might be enabled to share her faith with more young people. She found a way to fit the accident into the framework of religious belief that she had already accepted as a teenager.[9] By contrast, Rabbi Kushner found that he was unable to deal with his son's rare disease through his inherited religious categories. He could not accept the notion that Aaron's illness and death were God's will, so he had to reconstruct his theology around those elements of his faith that he was able to hold onto. At the end of his book he acknowledges that the agony of that experience did make him a more sympathetic counselor and did multiply the number of people he was reaching a thousandfold. All that, however, did not alter the tragedy of Aaron's death for him or turn it into God's will for his life. "I would give up all of those gains in a second if I could have my son back," he says.[10]

Different from either Joni Eareckson or Rabbi Kushner was the way of rebuilding faith adopted by Ella, the woman whose husband was critically injured in a traffic accident. During the first week he nearly died, but he rallied and recovered to a degree that exceeded even his doctors' wildest hopes. Friends began to talk about his rehabilitation as "miraculous." To his family it was not exactly a miracle, however, for the severe brain damage caused by the accident resulted in a changed personality. So different was he that his adolescent daughter refused to consider him her father. Ella never blamed God for what had happened, but she wrestled with the question of why God had allowed it. Three years after the accident she came to a kind of resolution. "I'm much more willing to take things on faith," she said. "I used to think I needed to know more answers, but now I'm realizing that life is full of things that don't have answers, and we can live very effectively and creatively and honestly within that."[11]

The responses of Joseph and Julia Quinlan were different yet, and different from each other as well.[12] Their differing reactions to the loss of the same child remind us how much our responses to a traumatic event depend upon what we bring to that event. Julie Quinlan was always the more accepting of the two, seemingly able to place the tragedy of Karen Ann in the context of her Catholic faith and practice and leave it to God. Joe, on the other hand, was dogged by the "why" question. He had to find a reason why this had happened to Karen. By the time their case went to court to determine whether or not Karen could be taken off the respirator, he had worked it out in his own mind. He had concluded that this tragedy happened to Karen in order to show the world that it was ethically right to refuse extraordinary means and allow a person to die naturally, "in God's own time." He was certain that when the court rendered its verdict and Karen was taken off the respirator, God would allow her to die.

The Quinlans won the court case and the respirator was turned off, but the unanticipated happened — Karen continued breathing on her own. Now Joe was thrown into a new faith crisis. If that wasn't the meaning of Karen's tragedy, what was? Although Joe never completely abandoned his earlier explanation, he and Julie themselves took a step that put Karen's loss into a context of meaning that redeemed the tragedy for them. They decided to let Karen's story be told in print and subsequently on television, with the proceeds used to build a hospice named "The Karen Ann Quinlan Center of Hope."

Phase Three: Changing

In making that step the Quinlans were really moving into the third phase, which I call "changing." They were taking action to redeem the meaning of the tragic event through their own creative initiative, albeit in harmony with the will of God as they saw it. Sometimes it is not possible to go beyond the phase-two task of learning to live with things as they are. In some situations, that is the best one can do. More often, however, it is possible to move toward significant change, either in ourselves or in the circumstances, in a way that is transforming as well as redeeming. The Quinlans could not change the fact of Karen's irreversible vegetative state, but they did change the world around them both through a landmark court decision and through the creation of a new health facility. In doing so, they were moving beyond survival toward the kind of transformation that marks phase three.

Sometimes one changes oneself rather than the environing world. After her husband's accident, Ella engaged the best therapists to help her injured husband recover as much of his mental capacity as possible, but eventually therapy reached a plateau and could go no further. Then she had to change her own thinking and attitudes, and that she did. She also had to invent a whole new pattern of social life, in which she included her husband in those things he could still enjoy, such as concerts and plays, and participated in other social events as a single adult. Hugh Herr and Jeff Batzer, the two climbers trapped on Mt. Washington, lost their fight to save their limbs, but Hugh found a way to return to mountain climbing with artificial legs, and Jeff discovered in bicycle racing a substitute for the excitement he formerly derived from climbing.

As persons begin to take charge of their own lives, a more active attitude replaces the reactive stance of the impact phase. The new sense of power can be exhilarating; yet changing is hard work that brings with it its own kind of suffering, as Sölle attests:

> This process itself is painful. At first it intensifies suffering and strips away whatever camouflaged it.... The suffering is now looked at carefully, it is taken seriously, and only under these conditions can the new question arise, How do I organize to conquer suffering?[13]

Every formerly married person knows how difficult it is to begin dating all over again or to build relationships in some alternative way. The unemployed person, moving on to a new job, must learn new skills and may have to learn to live on a reduced income. More painful yet, some persons discover within themselves obstacles that must be removed in order to move forward in life. The midwifing assistance of others is essential if such "new birth" is to come about. In this phase (as in the previous ones) the depth of hurt and the pace of healing will depend greatly on social attitudes toward the particular affliction. In North Vietnam, Sölle observes, the anguish of individual suffering was assuaged by the strong public support for the Vietnamese cause.

The thousand-year history of resistance to foreign oppression and the conviction that necessary sacrifices were worthwhile put individual suffering in the transcendent framework that Cassell considers so important. Sölle might have contrasted that with the situation in the U.S. Our confusion and dispute over the war and its aims, our sense that in the end it was all a meaningless waste, and our failure to acknowledge the sacrifices made on our behalf by those who did the fighting, have made it extremely difficult to heal the psychological wounds and bring to an end the suffering of those who fought in the war.

It is not difficult to find other examples where social disapproval heightens the anguish and slows the healing process. Consider the plight of the divorced. Those who counsel divorcing persons know that even with our more liberal attitudes today, most persons who dissolve their marriages feel shame and guilt — shame because divorce symbolizes failure, and guilt because a vow made before God and the community has been broken. No matter how impossible the marriage may have been, its dissolution leaves an indelible smudge on divorcing persons' lives. They feel "stained" in the eyes of others, and the sense of isolation is greater than with many other forms of affliction. Some find it difficult to continue going to church because of community disapproval, real or imagined. It is easier to be a widow or widower than divorced, many say.

But the most extreme example today is the social ostracism of persons with AIDS, that modern equivalent of the bubonic plague. We have all read the frightful stories about AIDS victims rejected by their families, ejected from their apartments, and without anyone willing to care for them. Communities panic when children with AIDS — often children who are already suffering from hemophilia — seek to attend the public school. Too frequently the result is ostracism and even the necessity to pull up roots and move elsewhere. The horror of such situations staggers the imagination; and yet the taboo surrounding AIDS is strong enough to make most of us hesitate. Sölle asks whether the church is on the side of the victim or the oppressor. We have much work to do before we can honestly say that in this situation, the church is on the side of the victim.

Resistance

Throughout the sweep of Christian history, compassionate ministry to hurting persons has been an essential dimension of the church's mission and a basic responsibility of each member. Yet ministering to the afflicted is by itself an inadequate response wherever it is possible to eliminate the source of that affliction or diminish its efficacy. If a dangerous intersection is causing traffic accidents, we cannot content ourselves with aiding the injured; we need to confront "city hall" to get the problem corrected. The point seems obvious, but Christians are slow to act on its implications. For instance, congregations that sense the urgent need to shelter and feed the homeless often hesitate to advocate political action to remedy the causes of homelessness. Yet the people of God are called not only "to bind up the brokenhearted" and "comfort all who mourn"; they are also called "to proclaim liberty to the captives, and the opening of the prison to those who are bound" (Isa. 61:1–2). Working toward justice in human society is part of the faithful response to the God who declares, "Let justice roll down like waters."

Biblical faith is thus inescapably political. Religions that are as deeply ethical as Judaism and Christianity can never settle for a truncated gospel that separates religion from social action. Empathic response to the *pathos* of God will lead God's people to utilize constituted processes for change in order to reduce human suffering and establish justice. Sometimes, however, injustice is so deeply entrenched that it will not yield to "due process." It is in such circumstances that the question arises of the means to be used to resist the powers of evil.

It may be objected that in the Sermon on the Mount Jesus has commanded nonresistance: "Do not resist one who is evil" (Matt. 5:39). That sounds like an instruction to remain passive in the face of evil. It is a puzzling exhortation in light of Jesus' own confrontative words and actions throughout his ministry.

This is one of those instances in which the translation from Greek to English has led us into serious misunderstanding. Walter Wink points out that the Greek *antistenai,* rendered as "resist not" in the King James translation and "do not resist" in the Revised Standard Version, is constructed from a Greek stem referring to violent rebellion or armed revolt. Thus a more precise translation would be, "Do not take up arms against evil," or

"Do not engage in violent rebellion against one who is evil."[14] Jesus is not, then, ordering his followers to be passive, but to eschew violence as a way of responding to evil. Christian resistance must take another form.

The familiar admonitions that follow this command make Jesus' intention clearer.

> But if anyone strikes you on the right cheek, turn to him the other also; and if anyone would sue you and take your coat, let him have your cloak as well; and if any one forces you to go one mile, go with him two miles. (Matt. 5:39–41)

When read in the context of the laws and customs prevailing in first-century Palestine, Jesus' three exhortations are creative alternatives to passive obedience on the one hand or foolhardy rebellion on the other, claims Wink. Far from being passive submission, the proposed actions go beyond compliance by seizing the initiative, lampooning and embarrassing the oppressor, highlighting the injustice, and restoring dignity to the oppressed. For instance, a backhand slap to the right cheek was the customary way to humiliate an inferior, putting the upstart in his or her place. Custom dictated that this had to be done with the back of the right hand, which means that the right cheek would be struck. Thus turning the *left* cheek would surprise the superior and present an embarrassing problem: how do you slap a person on the left cheek with the back of the right hand? In that culture turning the other cheek was a daring act, asserting the dignity of the oppressed at some considerable risk. Wink calls this "Jesus' Third Way," because this form of nonviolent resistance finds a creative alternative to the two instinctive responses of "fight or flight."[15]

Wink is surely correct in identifying creative nonviolence as the preferred means for resisting evil in the Christian community. It was the sole acceptable mode of resistance during the first three centuries of the Christian church, which regarded nonviolence as the only stance consistent with the sixth commandment, "Thou shalt not kill," and with the teachings of Jesus. Even the concept of the just war, which eventually became the dominant policy of Catholics and Protestants alike, recognized nonviolence as the norm for Christians and placed the burden of proof on those who would take up arms.[16]

Nonviolence is both a theological stance and a political strategy. As a faith stance, creative nonviolence is a reflection of the creative power of God that works through persuasion rather than coercion. It is, further, a mode of action that recognizes all persons as created in the image of God and therefore to be loved, even as God loves them. Ever since Peter, one of the most difficult injunctions for Christians is "Love your enemies" — a divine command that stands as a constant obstacle to any demonizing "enemy creation." Consistent with this, the community that embraces nonviolence ultimately seeks reconciliation with its foes in the struggle, no matter how conflictive the resistance may become. Those committed to nonviolence also recognize that healing usually requires suffering, even as God suffers with us for our healing, and follow their Lord in taking that suffering on themselves instead of inflicting it on their opponents. Finally, nonviolence respects the importance of order by willingly accepting the legal consequences of disobedience, even when the laws are unjust.

As a faith stance, nonviolence is embraced regardless of its success or failure, but as a strategy it will be employed only so long as it holds greater promise of success than alternative strategies. Reinhold Niebuhr, no friend of pacifism and a realist regarding power, supported nonviolence as an appropriate strategy for the Civil Rights movement: "I would honor the principle of nonviolence, not for purely moral reasons,... but because it is pragmatically the only way that a minority group can deal with a majority group."[17]

The nonviolent strategy is to confront coercive force with a different combination of power. One aspect of this will be moral authority. Certainly nonviolent resistance must claim the ethical high ground if it is to be a successful strategy, for nonviolence will never win against coercive force if it is perceived to be operating on the same moral level. Yet it would be sentimental to believe that moral suasion alone could be successful. The just cause must be embodied in a sizable and disciplined community willing to accept sacrifices to achieve its goal. By working together in solidarity, people who once regarded themselves as powerless discover their own strength. The strategy also calls for creative invention (itself a reflection of the divine), but creative alternatives require more effort than the instinctive reflexes of "fight or flight."

Nonviolence as a strategy might logically be abandoned if it does not achieve its goal in a reasonable period of time. As a theological mandate for the Christian community, however, it remains normative regardless of the outcome, and any shift to a strategy involving violence would have to be justified as a reasonable deviation from that norm.

The movements led by Gandhi and Martin Luther King, Jr., are familiar and impressive illustrations of nonviolence as both stance and strategy. A less familiar but scarcely less striking example was provided by the French village of Le Chambon during World War II. This remarkable story was brought to light in 1979 by the publication of Philip Hallie's *Lest Innocent Blood Be Shed.* For years ethicist Hallie had been researching the nature of cruelty, reading document after document on Hitler's death camps, until he had become embittered and numbed toward the very evil he was investigating. Then unexpectedly he stumbled across a brief report of what had transpired in Le Chambon. Moved to tears by this account of how a Reformed congregation had mobilized the entire community to hide thousands of Jews from the advancing Nazi tide, Hallie shifted his research to the documenting and retelling of that tale. Hence the subtitle of his book: *The Story of the Village of Le Chambon and How Goodness Happened There.*

Hallie's account is also the life story of Le Chambon's pastor, André Trocmé, who during those years became known as "the soul of Le Chambon." Although nonviolence was not a part of Trocmé's French Reformed heritage, his childhood experiences of violence in his family and in the war-torn city of his origin (only twenty miles from the Battle of the Somme) taught him the preciousness of all human life and the fruitlessness of the vicious circle of revenge. Trocmé's commitment to nonviolence was a simple attitude toward people and a decision to "stay close to Jesus" and to "love your enemies" as Jesus had taught. It had nothing to do with Trocmé's natural temperament, for he was "a violent man conquered by God," as he and his friends alike said.[18]

In 1934 Trocmé was called to be the pastor of the Reformed Temple in Le Chambon, a village whose location in the mountains of southern France had made it a Huguenot refuge in the seventeenth century and a summer resort in the twentieth. On his arrival Trocmé found the village "dead" and its attitude one of resignation: "There's nothing you can do."[19] Trocmé refused to accept that, however. In addition to visiting tirelessly from house to house he organized the parish into thirteen Bible study groups, each with its own *responsable,* or leader. The pastor met regularly with the *responsables* to study the texts and discern their practical relevance for the lives of the people.

A second project instituted by Trocmé was the founding of Cévenol, a secondary school organized to educate an international student body in the way of nonviolence, even as war clouds were gathering over Europe. Pastor Édouard Theiss was called to direct the school and assist Trocmé in the parish. Other key leaders in the parish were Roger Darcissac, headmaster of the public Boys' School, situated across the road from the Temple, and Trocmé's wife, Magda.

France fell quickly to the German *Blitzkrieg* in the summer of 1940, and the leaders of defeated Vichy France promptly adopted National Socialism's *Führer* principle and anti-Semitic ideology. During this time Trocmé and Theiss preached that resistance to evil must cherish the value of all persons, even one's adversaries, and must oppose the destruction of any human life. Trocmé was convinced that occasions for practicing nonviolent resistance would soon open up and counseled a canny watchfulness for opportunities to implement it.[20]

Opportunities soon came. When school opened in the fall, the Vichy government required that each school erect a large flagpole and begin each day with a salute to the flag, performed in stiff-armed, fascist style. To Trocmé this gesture signified surrender of one's conscience. Darcissac came up with a creative solution. Each morning the students in his school, which as a state institution had no choice but to comply, formed a semicircle around their flagpole that stood beside the road just across from the Cévenol School. Those from Cévenol who wished to join in the salute were invited to complete the circle and perform the salute from their side of the road. At first a few students and one professor participated in this manner. Gradually their numbers diminished, until after a few weeks no one any longer participated, on either side of the road. If the government took no notice, the three thousand inhabitants of Le Chambon did. The incident may seem trivial, but its symbolic significance was great, signaling to the villagers that resistance was possible.[21]

A second opportunity for symbolic resistance presented itself when the mayor issued an order to ring all church bells at noon on the anniversary of Marshal Pétain's founding of the French Legion. This was intended to show gratitude to the marshal for the discipline and pride he had brought to the "soul" of France. Trocmé instructed the custodian of the Temple not to comply. On the appointed day two prominent ladies appeared at the Temple and insisted that the bell be rung. The custodian refused, saying, "The bell does not belong to the marshal, but to God. It is rung for God — otherwise it is not rung."[22]

A third occasion was the visit to Le Chambon of the Vichy minister of youth, Georges Lamirand. This occurred shortly after the massacre of Jews at the Vélodrome d'Hiver in Paris in 1942. A dozen Cévenol students used the occasion to present Lamirand with a letter of protest, including the following paragraphs:

> We feel obliged to tell you that there are among us a certain number of Jews. But, we make no distinction between Jews and non-Jews. It is contrary to the Gospel teaching.
>
> If our comrades, whose only fault is to be born in another religion, received the order to let themselves be deported, or even examined, they would disobey the orders received, and we would try to hide them as best we could.[23]

After reading the letter, Lamirand, his face ashen, made a hasty exit, leaving the matter in the hands of the prefect of the district of Haute-Loire, in which Le Chambon was situated. The prefect scolded Trocmé: "This day should be a day of national harmony. You sow division."

Trocmé answered, "It cannot be a question of national harmony when our brothers are threatened with deportation."

"Foreign Jews who live in the Haute-Loire are not your brothers," the official retorted, drawing on the ploy of enemy-creation. "The Führer has ordered the regrouping of all European Jews in Poland.... In a few days my people will come to examine the Jews living in Le Chambon."

"We do not know what a Jew is," Trocmé shot back. "We know only men."[24] By this time the village was already deeply involved in hiding Jews. There had been no deliberate plan to do this. It had simply resulted from "canny watchfulness for opportunity," as refugees fleeing the advance of Nazism began appearing in large numbers. In the winter of 1941, when an ill-clad Jewish woman with hunger written on her face stood in the snow before the Trocmés' door, Magda decided that turning away such a person would be more than refusing to help; it would be harmdoing and therefore evil. After that there was a constant stream of Jewish refugees through her house — more than sixty in the course of one summer alone.

As the project of hiding refugees gradually took shape, the church council gave its approval. The Bible study groups and their *responsables* provided the organization and communications network for this "kitchen struggle." Darcissac found a way to furnish refugees with false identity and ration cards — a measure difficult to accept for these French Protestants who prized honesty. Houses that had rented rooms to tourists now provided space for refugees, and outlying farmers offered more secure hiding places when needed. The last resort was a ski team that undertook the dangerous task of escorting refugees to the Swiss border.

Two weeks after the confrontation with Lamirand, the prefect of Haute-Loire carried out his promise. On a Saturday night the chief of police appeared in the village square, accompanied by two khaki-colored buses and a contingent of motorcycle police. Trocmé was summoned and ordered to turn over the names and addresses of all Jews hidden in the district. He replied that he did not know their names (he knew only the pseudonyms on their identity cards), and that even if he did, he would not disclose them. "It is not the role of a shepherd to betray the sheep confided to his keeping," he said. The chief of police angrily delivered an ultimatum to turn over his Jews by the next morning.

Trocmé quickly dispatched the Boy Scouts and *responsables* to alert those endangered and to put into operation the plan for concealing Jews in outlying farms and forests. The next morning the Temple was packed and tense. From the high pulpit the pastors preached on the text, "We must obey God rather than men" (Acts 5:29). They exhorted their people to live an active, dangerous love, giving help to those who need it most.

By the time the service was over, the police had already begun a house-to-house search. The dragnet was gradually extended to the surrounding countryside. Only one unfortunate refugee was ensnared, and he had to be released when it was discovered that he was only half Jewish.[25] Six months later police returned to arrest Trocmé himself. The pastor was out calling in the parish, so Magda invited the arresting officers to make themselves at home while they waited, even persuading them to have dinner with the family. After dinner the officers escorted Trocmé to a half-track waiting in the town square, as his parishioners, who were by then lining the streets, began singing "A Mighty Fortress Is Our God." Theiss and Darcissac were also arrested. The three were released after a month in a French concentration camp, during which they held evangelistic services for the communists with whom they shared the camp.[26]

Not all their efforts to resist ended so successfully. In the summer of 1943 the Gestapo raided the House of the Rocks, which had been established as a sanctuary for Jewish children using funds donated by the American Friends Service Committee. Despite Magda's cleverest attempts to intervene, three busloads of children, together with their headmaster, Daniel Trocmé (André's cousin), were carried away to the gas chambers in Maidanek.[27] Nevertheless, by the end of the war thousands of Jews had been spared a similar fate through the efforts of the people of Le Chambon.

In the story of Le Chambon we find numerous key elements of any program of nonviolent resistance: a well-focused purpose and a rationale that gave the effort meaning; a community educated in nonviolence and strengthened by solidarity; actions that seized the moral initiative by confronting oppression; love and respect for all persons, including both strangers and foes; creative strategies and symbolic actions; readiness to suffer violence rather than inflict it; and willingness to accept the legal consequences of one's actions.

It is an inspiring tale of a small village that risked its own safety to save the lives of others. Dare we generalize from this story? May we conclude that Le Chambon shows us in microcosm how Christians might have opposed Hitler? Even more broadly, is this a blueprint for resisting evil in any and all situations?

Hallie himself has pondered that question as he reflected on the contradictions in his own life. During World War II he was an artilleryman, pounding German lines with phosphorus shells and afterward seeing the heads and limbs of German boys dismembered by those shells. "I see the heads, especially those heads, the beautiful young people," he recalls. "If that's not evil, there's no such thing." After the war he focused his professional research on cruelty while holding fast to the preciousness of human life. In mid-career he discovered the story "about the way this little village saved people's lives without killing or hurting or hating anybody." It changed the direction of his life.

> So I wrote *Lest Innocent Blood Be Shed,* and became converted, a different person of sorts, for a while. And then I said to myself, "Wait a minute.... Something in your heart resents the village.... They didn't stop Hitler. They did nothing to stop Hitler...."
>
> A thousand Le Chambons would not have stopped Hitler. It took decent murderers like me to do it. Murderers who had compunctions, but who murdered nonetheless to stop him. The cruelty that I perpetrated willingly was the only way to stop the cruel march that I and others like me were facing.... And the paradox ... is that I am a decent murderer, that I am a conscientious killer, I am somebody who would do it again if I were in similar circumstances, and I wouldn't hesitate to do it again.[28]

Hallie's impassioned defense is recognizable as the rationale for just war.

Scott Peck struggles to resolve the same dilemma. War, he insists, is always a failure, resulting from bad choices. "Whenever war is waged, some human beings have lost their moorings.... A wrong choice has been made somewhere."[29] Furthermore, the attempt to destroy evil with evil only fuels a vicious circle.

> If we kill those who are evil, we will become evil ourselves; we will be killers. If we attempt to deal with evil by destroying it, we will also end up destroying ourselves, spiritually if not physically. And we are likely to take some innocent people with us as well.[30]

All this is abundantly illustrated by the Vietnam conflict. Peck concludes that evil cannot be defeated by evil, only by goodness. "Evil can be conquered only by love."[31] Yet finally Peck draws back from making that into an absolute principle:

It is personally extremely tempting for me to think sim-
plistically about war. I would like to take the Sixth Commandment literally, to believe that "Thou shalt not kill"
means just that.... But thus far I cannot escape the conclusion that in rare previous moments of human history it
has been necessary and morally right to kill in order to prevent even greater killing. I am profoundly uncomfortable
with this position.[32]

I agree with Peck that there have been "rare moments" when the
resort to arms has been justified. Hitler may well have provided
one of these moments, and I cannot rule out the possibility that
such a moment may arise again. Even if we acknowledge that,
however, we must not lose sight of Peck's observations that war
always represents failure, and that social dynamics (such as national narcissism) push us toward using force as the preferred
means for solving problems instead of a last resort. One must
ask, further, whether the emergence of total war, guerrilla tac-
tics, and nuclear weapons have not made the criteria for a just
war impossible to fulfil in the present age.[33] Indeed, it seems
that war itself, in its classic definition as "diplomacy carried
on by other means," has become obsolete — a fact humankind
seems slow to recognize. Thus it is incumbent upon Christians,
now more than ever as the twentieth century draws to a close,
to cultivate our neglected tradition of creative nonviolence.

Liturgy

Our examination of personal presence and corporate resistance
has focused on horizontal relationships between persons and
groups, although the people of God know that the "vertical"
is always also present. God is the "between" in relationships, to
use Buber's insightful metaphor. The liturgy makes this implicit
presence of God explicit in word and action. By liturgy, which
etymologically refers to "the work of the people," I mean the
worship of the church, including its praise and prayers, sacra-
ments and scriptures, sermons and songs. The liturgy embodies
and enacts the healing touch of the divine transcendence, surrounding life with meaning and giving it hope.

All of us old enough to remember it know exactly where we
were at the time of John Kennedy's assassination, and also re-

member the feelings of disbelief, anguish, and confusion that swept over us in that awful moment. I was a chaplain at the University of Maryland at the time. It was a Friday, and we had a graduate group meeting scheduled for that evening. We considered cancelling it, but the group said no, they wanted to be together. So they gathered at our home, shared a meal, talked quietly, and played some music, as I recall. The Sunday following I had to be in New York. I remember my sense of relief that it wasn't my turn to lead chapel, because I felt empty-handed, devoid of anything worth saying. In the back of my head was the notion that if I just had enough faith and intelligence, I would be able to come up with something profound that would shed light or meaning on this tragedy. I also recall that it was very important for me personally to attend service that Sunday in New York, but I don't remember what words were spoken.

It was only much later that I was helped to understand all this by Jim Anderson, now dean of the College of the Laity at the Washington Cathedral. He had been a parish priest at the time, and he recollects that the services at his church, as everywhere, were packed. People, he said, did not come because they were looking for an explanation, for who could possibly unravel the mystery of such a happening? Rather, they came to set this event within the divine drama that sustains the meaningfulness and worth of human existence, beyond our ability to explain. It was then that I came to realize that all our attempts at rational explanations of ultimate meaning rest on dramas and stories and myths that transcend rational meaning and give reason its presuppositions. Those of us who are academicians, and those of us who are Protestants, are too prone to restrict reality to that which we can formulate in logical, conceptual, verbal statements, when in truth our brains and our mouths represent only a fraction of our wholeness. That's why liturgy, sacrament, and ritual are so important to the sense of life's wholeness and worthwhileness.

Julia Quinlan recalls a special mass that was held in her church to give her family support on the eve of the court hearing that would decide whether or not Karen's respirator could be disconnected. Every seat in the chapel was filled, she remembers. Following a program of guitar music and singing, Father Trepasso celebrated mass, offering up Karen's life to God and asking for people's love. Afterward Julie reflected,

That night was such an exemplification of charity and love
— they were really reaching out to Joe and me, they really loved us.... The faith healers are always talking about
"miracles," about how they're going to go in and just raise
Karen up.... Miracles are done very quietly and very pri-
vately, and I believe this night was one. To see all those
people come in, and fill the church and just pour out their
love in prayer — that is a miracle.

We went to bed almost happy that night.[34]

Some will say that the power of this event was in the supportive
fellowship of so many well-wishers, but I think that misses the
added dimension. It would not have been the same if it had
been a public event in a lodge hall. This was the mass, and here
was the offering of prayers for Karen and the community, and
the offering of God's love, incarnated not only in the bread and
wine but also in the whole body of believers.

A few years ago when my wife, Jean, and I were leading a
church retreat, we met Rachel, who told us this story. Rachel's
son, Robert, and her daughter-in-law, Ann, had been married for
six years, but without children. Naturally Rachel was delighted
when they told her that she was about to become a grandmother.
She was even more elated when Geoffrey was born the following summer. Her joy lasted only a few days, however, for it
was soon discovered that Geoffrey had Down's Syndrome, and
a short time afterward, that he had a heart defect necessitat-
ing surgery. Geoffrey was baptized in the Sunday service of the
church to which Robert and Ann belonged. It was for Rachel a
deeply moving event in which their whole family was involved.
Communion was celebrated, and in his sermon, the pastor, making special reference to Geoffrey, spoke about the worth of every
person.

Shortly before Christmas Geoffrey died. It was a difficult
holiday for the family. All during this time the people of the
church were very supportive. Robert's work took him on the
road a lot, but the people saw to it that Ann was not left alone.
"I cannot tell you," said Rachel, "how much this support of the
church people meant to them in their grieving process and in
making the adjustment to lead a new life."

Some months later Ann announced that she was pregnant
again, and in due time a healthy daughter was born. It was

a very happy event, not only in the life of this young couple and grandmother, but in the life of the church as well. Here is Rachel's description of that relationship:

> She is a very special child in that church. They showered them with love, and they showered them with gifts. And I think the culmination of all that was at the time of her christening, when the minister stayed up half of the night before to make a banner which said, "Hip-hip hooray. Today is Karen's christening day!" This was carried down the aisle of the church in front of her as she and the family walked down. And then the whole family participated in the communion service after she was baptized. I can't tell you the joy that she has brought to our family.[35]

Some may wish to quarrel with this or that piece of the liturgical action in this story. The important thing is that here death and life were set within the context of a caring community and a compassionate God, symbolized and celebrated as dramatically and concretely as can be imagined. Neither words alone nor deeds alone can communicate the depth of meaning expressed here through liturgical action.

A similar power in a dissimilar setting was revealed when the liturgy was celebrated in the refugee camp at La Virtud, Honduras. In chapter 1, I told the story of Yvonne Dilling's experience as a volunteer worker among the Salvadoran refugees at La Virtud. In the midst of the disruption, loss, illness, and danger that marked life in the camp, Yvonne — Protestant, affluent, white — celebrated a Roman Catholic Easter with penniless brown refugees. There was not even a priest present to celebrate mass — only a lay catechist to lead the people in their liturgy. Just a month after the river crossing, the refugees gathered at 3:30 in the morning to watch with the three Marys during their hours of despair before the dawn. In the darkness they raised songs of mourning and distress. Yvonne recorded in her journal what ensued.

> At about 4:30 a liturgy began. First they elaborated on their own suffering: three children a day have died of diarrhea and dehydration this past week. Many are sick with

parasites, cough, headaches. "We are strangers expelled from our land by foreign forces," they said....

But for these people suffering and resurrection are not a matter of the past. "How is Jesus resurrected in us?" the catechist persists. Finally an old voice calls out, "Only if we carry on with his work of building a better world where justice dwells and suffering is ended."

Then follows the liturgy of light. It is almost dawn now, yet the trees shade us. From a central candle — the light of Jesus which is for all the world — candles are lit and passed one to another. With the passing, one says the name of a loved one "who has gone before us, following Jesus' example." For fifteen minutes the valley is filled with voices recalling the names of children, mothers, fathers, priests, nuns....

Then the candles return slowly to the center and are extinguished. The catechist says, "But look, the dawn has come!" Light surrounds us. We had not noticed it for the candles. But it is dawn, the stone is rolled away, the tomb cannot hold him. The power of death, so strong over these people, is broken. In struggle we shall overcome, we shall return home.[36]

When Christmas rolled around, Yvonne was again amazed by the ability of these poor people to celebrate amid misery and create a festival literally out of nothing. "Never have I experienced such a powerful Christmas celebration," she wrote in her diary.

At midnight the lay catechists led us in worship. Their simple, moving Christmas reflection was...that we are with Christ,...born in a strange town, forced to flee and take refuge in a foreign land at only three days of age. It was a sincere identification with Mary and Joseph and the new baby.[37]

When I first read Dilling's account of the profound suffering of these Salvadoran refugees, I wondered what it was that kept hope alive in the face of such tremendous adversity. Eventually it dawned on me that what enabled them to go on was the liturgy, which put these dreadful events in the context of a much more lasting and powerful force. Especially it was their ability to identify with the people of God in captivity and in exile, and with Jesus the refugee, the crucified, the resurrected one. They found their story in the biblical story, and that gave it a significance that no persecution could take away.

In that moment of discernment I came to a realization that I have been struggling to express ever since, because it defies all reason. Any human attempt to calculate the forces at work in that situation would have to conclude that this tattered flock of refugees were no match for the forces opposing them. I can readily imagine the army captain taunting the Catholic refugee workers with some Hispanic equivalent of Stalin's famous gibe, "How many divisions has the pope?" Yet I cannot shake the conviction that this disheveled band, with all the foolishness of their hope, are stronger than all the powers arrayed against them. In the weird logic of my imagination, I see them as an incarnation of Jesus' words: "In the world you have tribulation; but be of good cheer, I have overcome the world" (John 16:33).

Notes

1. "God It Hurts!":
Pain, Suffering, and the Threat to Human Meaning

1. Harold S. Kushner, *When Bad Things Happen to Good People* (New York: Schocken, 1981).
2. *Time,* July 6, 1981, p. 36.
3. *Intelligencer-Journal* (Lancaster, Pa.), September 8, 1978.
4. Eric J. Cassell, M.D., "The Nature of Suffering and the Goals of Medicine," *The New England Journal of Medicine* 306 (March 18, 1982), pp. 639–645.
5. Ibid., p. 640.
6. Ibid.
7. Ibid., p. 644.
8. Ibid., p. 640.
9. *Webster's New Universal Unabridged Dictionary,* Deluxe Second Edition (New York: Simon and Schuster, 1983).
10. Cassell, "The Nature of Suffering and the Goals of Medicine," p. 643.
11. Ibid., p. 641. Cf. Ronald Melzack and Patrick D. Wall, "Pain Mechanisms: A New Theory," *Science* 150 (November 19, 1965), pp. 971–979, in which the authors postulate a new "gate-control theory of pain" to account for the ways in which attention, memory, values, emotions, and other factors modulate the sensations transmitted physiologically through the neural system.
12. Cassell, "The Nature of Suffering and the Goals of Medicine," p. 643.
13. Yvonne Dilling with Ingrid Rogers, *In Search of Refuge* (Scottdale, Pa.: Herald Press, 1984).
14. *The Letters of John Keats,* ed. M. B. Forman, 4th ed. (London: Oxford University Press, 1952), pp. 334–335.
15. Walter Kaufman, *The Faith of a Heretic* (Garden City, N.Y.: Doubleday, 1961), p. 139.
16. Cassell, "The Nature of Suffering and the Goals of Medicine," p. 644.
17. Dorothee Sölle, *Suffering,* trans. Everett R. Kalin (Philadelphia: Fortress, 1975), pp. 85–86.
18. Rich Sander, "The Long Road Back: Rescued Climbers Year Later," *Intelligencer-Journal* (Lancaster, Pa.), February 2, 1983; Mary Jane Lane, "Jeff Batzer Returns to Conquer Mountain," *Sunday News* (Lancaster, Pa.), September 18, 1983; Ad Crable, "Crippled Climber Rebuilds Shattered Life 'Better than Before,'" *New Era* (Lancaster, Pa.), January 25, 1984.

2. "Why God?":
Omnipotence Reconsidered

1. "And justify the ways of God to men" is John Milton's oft-quoted definition of theodicy (*Paradise Lost,* 1, 26). Gabriel Fackre defines theodicy as "the question of how we hold together a belief in the power of God, the love of God and the reality of evil" (*The Christian Story: A Narrative Interpretation of Basic Christian Doctrine,* rev. ed. [Grand Rapids, Mich.: Eerdmans, 1984], p. 58).
2. *Webster's New Universal Unabridged Dictionary.*
3. Leander E. Keck, "A Word Among Us Theologians," *Reflection* 77 (November 1979), p. 5.
4. S. Paul Schilling, *God and Human Anguish* (Nashville: Abingdon, 1977), p. 10.
5. Philip Hallie, *Lest Innocent Blood Be Shed: The Story of the Village of Le Chambon and How Goodness Happened There* (New York: Harper & Row, 1979; Harper Colophon Books, 1980), pp. 22, 85.

6. Archibald MacLeish, *J.B.* (Boston: Houghton Mifflin, 1956), p. 11.

7. Elie Wiesel, *Night,* trans. Stella Rodway (New York: Hill & Wang, 1960; Discus Books, published by Avon, 1969), p. 78.

8. Joseph and Julia Quinlan, with Phyllis Battelle, *Karen Ann: The Quinlans Tell Their Story* (Garden City, N.Y.: Doubleday, 1977), pp. 94–95.

9. *Intelligencer-Journal* (Lancaster, Pa.), November 16, 1978.

10. Perhaps the contrast between the godly behavior of these five and "the way of the world" is a subtle questioning of the justice in this event.

11. Dewey J. Hoitenga, Jr., sets forth three conditions for a valid "greater good" argument: (1) the lesser evil permitted must be logically necessary in order to achieve the higher good; (2) the good achieved must "outweigh" the evil permitted, and (3) the value of the higher good must be greater than any alternative good that might be achieved without using the lesser evil as a means ("Logic and the Problem of Evil," *American Philosophical Quarterly* 4 [April 1967], pp. 114–126).

12. The perspectival nature of evil becomes even more apparent as we examine several definitions proposed by theologians writing on evil. Immediately following his definition, quoted above, Schilling adds, "It is not easy to distinguish between real and apparent goods and evils, though we dare never forget that events *perceived as evil by the one experiencing them* must be treated seriously because they are evil *for him*" (Schilling, *God and Human Anguish,* p. 10, emphasis added). The perspective of "the one experiencing them" is, however, too subjective for John Hick and David Ray Griffin. Hick defines good and evil from God's eye-view: "Whatever tends to promote the attainment of [the divine purpose] will be good and whatever tends to thwart it will be bad" (John Hick, *Evil and the God of Love* [London: Macmillan, 1966; Fontana Library 1968], p. 15). Griffin seeks an all-inclusive, impartial perspective without invoking God: "By 'genuine evil,' I mean anything, all things considered, without which the universe would have been better" (David Ray Griffin, *God, Power, and Evil: A Process Theodicy* [Philadelphia: Westminster, 1976], p. 22). Hick's and Griffin's definitions do not escape the perspectival issue but move it to another level, for what an interpreter believes to be the divine purpose depends on his or her perspective, as does that "without which the universe would have been better."

13. David R. Griffin makes exactly this critique of Stephen T. Davis's theodicy. "Davis is making his three propositions [our three premises] consistent by simply denying one of them" (*Encountering Evil: Live Options in Theodicy,* ed. Stephen T. Davis [Atlanta: John Knox, 1981], p. 89).

14. Alvin Plantinga, *God, Freedom, and Evil* (New York: Harper & Row, 1974), p. 30.

15. C. S. Lewis, *The Problem of Pain* (New York: Macmillan, 1940; Macmillan Paperbacks Edition, 1962), p. 29.

16. "God's omnipotence...means that God is omnicompetent, capable of dealing with all circumstances, that nothing can ultimately defeat or thwart his plan for his people" (Donald G. Bloesch, *Essentials of Evangelical Theology,* vol. 1, *God, Authority, and Salvation* [New York: Harper & Row, 1978], p. 28). "God is indeed all-powerful.... God's power is all-sufficient.... God has all the power needed to fulfill the divine purpose" (Fackre, *The Christian Story: A Narrative Interpretation of Basic Christian Doctrine,* p. 58).

17. It was precisely this sense of balanced forces that led M. Scott Peck to investigate the possible existence of an evil power: "Having come over the years to a belief in the reality of benign spirit, or God, and a belief in the reality of human evil, I was left facing an obvious intellectual question: Is there such a thing as evil spirit?" (*People of the Lie: The Hope for Healing Human Evil* [New York: Simon and Schuster, 1983], p. 182). Paul Ricoeur, however, insists that evil "is not symmetrical with the good;... it is the staining, the darkening, the disfiguring of an innocence, a light, and a beauty that remain. However radical

evil may be, it cannot be as primordial as goodness" (*The Symbolism of Evil,* trans. Emerson Buchanan [Boston: Beacon, 1967], pp. 156–157).

18. Ricoeur, *The Symbolism of Evil,* pp. 175–198. Ricoeur identifies four classic types of myth — theogonic, tragic, Adamic, and Orphic — each expressing a different interpretation of evil.

19. Edwin Lewis, *The Creator and the Adversary* (New York: Abingdon-Cokesbury, 1948), cited in Bernhard W. Anderson, *Creation Versus Chaos: The Reinterpretation of the Mythical Symbolism in the Bible* (Philadelphia: Fortress, 1987), p. 145,

20. Harold S. Kushner, *When Bad Things Happen to Good People* (New York: Schocken, 1981), pp. 46–55. Tracing the logic of the second law of thermodynamics, Kushner even entertains the possibility that it might be chaos that triumphs in the end (pp. 55–56).

21. Charles Hartshorne, "A New Look at the Problem of Evil," *Current Philosophical Issues: Essays in Honor of Curt John Ducasse,* comp. and ed. Frederick E. Dommeyer, Ph.D. (Springfield, Ill.: Charles C. Thomas, 1966), pp. 201–212; Griffin, *God, Power, and Evil,* chaps. 17 and 18.

22. William C. Tremmel claims that "the Evil One" is the more accurate translation (*Dark Side: The Satan Story* [St. Louis: CBP Press, 1987], p. 75).

23. Walter Wink highlights the New Testament texts in which Satan continues to function as a servant of God (*The Powers,* vol. 2, *Unmasking the Powers: The Invisible Forces that Determine Human Existence* [Philadelphia: Fortress, 1986], pp. 14–22).

24. Bernhard W. Anderson, *Creation versus Chaos,* p. 68.

25. A number of philosophers and theologians question whether divine omnipotence can be preserved by speaking of the limitation on God's power as merely "self-limitation." Process theologians claim that the very concept of God includes creativity as an essential attribute, in which case God cannot even be conceived without some world as concomitant. Hence the idea of God possessing all power is self-contradictory and nonsensical. See esp. Griffin, *God, Power, and Evil,* chap. 17, "Worshipfulness and the Omnipotence Fallacy." J. L. Mackie also speaks of the "Paradox of Omnipotence": "Can an omnipotent being make things which he cannot subsequently control? Or, what is practically equivalent to this, can an omnipotent being make rules which then bind himself?...If we answer 'Yes,' it follows that if God actually makes things which he cannot control, or makes rules which bind himself, he is not omnipotent once he had made them: there are *then* things which he cannot do. But if we answer 'No,' we are immediately asserting that there are things which he cannot do, that is to say that he is already not omnipotent" ("Evil and Omnipotence," *Mind* 64 [1955], reprinted in *The Power of God: Readings on Omnipotence and Evil,* ed. Linwood Urban and Douglas N. Walton [New York: Oxford University Press, 1978], pp. 28–29).

26. Kushner, *When Bad Things Happen to Good People,* p. 58.

27. S. V. McCasland, "Miracle," *The Interpreter's Dictionary of the Bible,* vol. 3 (Nashville: Abingdon, 1962), pp. 392–402.

28. Cf. Plantinga, *God, Freedom, and Evil,* esp. pp. 27–34. Plantinga himself distinguishes between a theodicy and a defense, using the latter term in a more restricted way to indicate merely a possible line of argument against the atheistic claim (pp. 27–28), but "Free-will Defense" has come to have a broader connotation.

29. C. S. Lewis, *The Problem of Pain,* p. 89.

30. *Newsweek,* March 10, 1980, p. 97. C. S. Lewis agrees with Wiesel on this, however. "Even if all suffering were man-made, we should like to know the reason for the enormous permission to torture their fellows which God gives to the worst of men" (Lewis, *The Problem of Pain,* p. 77).

31. *Ancient Christian Writers,* vol. 22, *The Problem of Free Choice* (Westminster, Md.: Newman, 1955), bk. 2, 15.

32. Douglas John Hall, *God & Human Suffering: An Exercise in the Theology of the Cross* (Minneapolis: Augsburg, 1986), pp. 70–71 (emphasis Hall's). Hall goes on to raise and answer a second objection: "How often and how fervently does the rational mind ask whether freedom is worth its cost! But biblical faith would not forfeit the freedom of this creature, even for a world order in which whatever suffering there were would always, automatically, serve the life process" (p. 71).

33. An exception is evangelical philosopher Michael Peterson: "Much pain and suffering comes from accidental or inadvertent actions" (*Evil and the Christian God* [Grand Rapids, Mich.: Baker Book House, 1982], p. 21).

34. The second Helvetic Confession, chap. VIII; the Westminster Confession, chap. VI, para. 4; cf. the Heidelberg Catechism, questions 5 and 8.

35. Walter Wink, *The Powers*, vol. 1, *Naming the Powers: The Language of Power in the New Testament* (Philadelphia: Fortress, 1984), p. ix.

36. Ibid., p. x.

3. "Where is God?":
Holiness Reconsidered

1. Elie Wiesel, *Night*, trans. Stella Rodway (New York: Hill & Wang, 1960; Discus Books, published by Avon, 1969), pp. 78, 79.

2. Cf. Pierre Wolff, *May I Hate God?* (New York: Paulist, 1979).

3. Elie Wiesel, *A Jew Today*, trans. Marion Wiesel (New York: Random House, 1978), p. 208.

4. John K. Roth, "A Theodicy of Protest" and "Roth's Response," in *Encountering Evil: Live Options in Theodicy*, ed. Stephen T. Davis (Atlanta: John Knox, 1981), pp. 7–22, 30–37.

5. Ibid., p. 19.

6. Ibid., p. 15.

7. Ibid., p. 14.

8. Ibid., p. 10.

9. Ibid., p. 11.

10. Ibid., p. 31.

11. Ibid.

12. Richard C. Bush et al., *The Religious World: Communities of Faith*, ed. Kyle M. Yates, Jr., 2nd ed. (New York: Macmillan, 1988), pp. 63–73.

13. Daniel J. Simundson, *Faith Under Fire: Biblical Interpretations of Suffering* (Minneapolis: Augsburg, 1980), pp. 17–41.

14. Jesus' twice-uttered call for repentance in Luke 13 retains a connection between suffering and sin, but the sin is universal and the predicted punishment is future rather than past. In John 9 the link between sin and affliction is severed, but not the connection between divine action and the man's blindness.

15. Erhard S. Gerstenberger and Wolfgang Schrage, *Suffering*, trans. John E. Steely (Nashville: Abingdon, 1980 [1977]), p. 227.

16. *We Hold These Truths: Documents of American Democracy*, ed. Stuart Gerry Brown (New York: Harper & Bros., 1941), p. 231.

17. H. Richard Niebuhr, "War as the Judgment of God," *Christian Century* 59 (May 13, 1941), pp. 630–633.

18. A different nuance of the proverb is brought out in the NEB: "The meltingpot is for silver and the crucible is for gold, but it is the Lord who assays hearts of men."

19. Gerstenberger and Schrage, *Suffering*, p. 217. Schrage does, however, find a refining and purifying motif in Ps. 12:6 and 66:10, and in Rev. 3:18.

20. Ibid.

21. Cf. ibid., pp. 110–113, 231–235.

22. John Hick, *Evil and the God of Love* (London: Macmillan, 1966; Fontana Library 1968). A lucid and succinct summary of his theodicy is also presented in Hick, "An Irenaean Theodicy" and "Hick's Response to Critiques," in *Encountering Evil: Live Options in Theodicy,* ed. Stephen T. Davis (Atlanta: John Knox, 1981), pp. 39–52, 63–68.

23. This is Hick's repeated way of stating the omnipotence and perfect goodness of God the creator.

24. Hick, "An Irenaean Theodicy," p. 39.

25. Ibid., p. 44.

26. Ibid., p. 50.

27. Ibid., p. 48.

28. Ibid., p. 49.

29. Ibid., p. 51; from Erich Fromm, "Values, Psychology, and Human Existence," *New Knowledge of Human Values,* ed. A. H. Maslow (New York: Harper, 1959), p. 156.

30. Ibid.

31. William Shakespeare, *Hamlet,* act II, scene 2, line 256.

32. William James, *The Varieties of Religious Experience: A Study in Human Nature* (New York: Longmans, Green, 1919 [1902]), pp. 88–89. This does not represent James's comprehensive view of evil, however.

33. *The Religious World,* pp. 77–79.

34. Edward Conze, *Buddhism: Its Essence and Development* (Oxford: Bruno Cassirer, 1951; New York: Harper & Row, Harper Torchbooks, 1959), p. 18.

35. Mary Baker Eddy, *Science and Health with Key to the Scriptures* (Boston: Trustees Under the Will of Mary Baker G. Eddy, 1934 [1875]), p. 110.

36. William Brandon, *The Last Americans* (New York: McGraw-Hill, 1974), p. 202.

37. Alexander Pope, *An Essay on Man,* Epistle 1, lines 289–294.

38. Catherine Marshall, *A Man Called Peter: The Story of Peter Marshall* (New York: McGraw-Hill, 1951), p. 259.

39. Ibid., p. 260.

40. Harold S. Kushner, *When Bad Things Happen to Good People* (New York: Schocken, 1981), p. 133.

41. Cited in Jürgen Moltmann, *Hope and Planning,* trans. Margaret Clarkson (New York: Harper & Row, 1971), p. 32.

42. Alan Paton, "The Nature and Ground of Christian Hope Today," in Paton, *Knocking on the Door: Shorter Writings,* ed. Colin Gardner (New York: Charles Scribner's Sons, 1975), p. 286.

43. William Shakespeare, *Hamlet,* act 1, scene 5, lines 166–167.

44. Robert Jay Lifton, *The Nazi Doctors: Medical Killing and the Psychology of Genocide* (New York: Basic Books, 1986), p. 13.

45. Hick, "An Irenaean Theodicy," p. 47.

46. *The Notebooks of Simone Weil* (London: Routledge and Kegan Paul, 1956), p. 294.

47. Hick, *Evil and the God of Love,* p. ix.

48. The Heidelberg Catechism, question 5.

49. Simundson, *Faith Under Fire,* p. 24.

4. "The Devil Made Me Do It": Demonic Power and Human Responsibility

1. "Facing Evil with Bill Moyers," a co-production of Public Affairs Television, Inc. and KERA/Dallas, March 28, 1988.

2. *Newsweek,* May 30, 1988, p. 56.

3. Cf. Hick: "The Christian concept of God's purpose for man enables the two kinds of evil — sin and suffering — to be bracketed together under their common contrariety to the divine purpose" (John Hick, *Evil and the God of Love* [London: Macmillan, 1966; Fontana Library 1968], p. 16).

4. M. Scott Peck, M.D., *People of the Lie: The Hope for Healing Human Evil* (New York: Simon and Schuster, 1983), p. 43.

5. Walter Wink, *The Powers,* vol. 2, *Unmasking the Powers: The Invisible Forces that Determine Human Existence* (Philadelphia: Fortress, 1986), p. 9.

6. William Calloley Tremell, *The Dark Side: The Satan Story* (St. Louis: CBP Press, 1987), p. 149.

7. Wink, *Unmasking the Powers,* p. 1.

8. James Harvey Robinson, *An Introduction to the History of Western Europe,* rev. and enl. by James T. Shotwell (Boston: Ginn and Company, 1946), pp. 162–164.

9. Anne Frank, *The Diary of a Young Girl* (New York: Doubleday, 1952; Pocket Books, 1953), p. 233.

10. The senseless slaughter of the world's youth in World War I is well-captured in Peter Weir's film *Gallipoli.*

11. Raul Hilberg represents a large consensus in stating, "In searching for good and evil, to put it very bluntly, one found the Holocaust a signpost, a marker: this is it" ("Facing Evil with Bill Moyers").

12. On "Walter Cronkite at Large," June 5, 1988, Barry Commoner and Paul Ehrlich reported five trends that could soon lead to a point of no return if not quickly reversed: the "greenhouse effect," ozone depletion, acid rain, toxic waste, and overpopulation.

13. Clyde Z. Nunn, "The Rising Credibility of the Devil in America," *Listening: Journal of Religion and Culture* 9 (1974), pp. 84–100.

14. "Facing Evil with Bill Moyers."

15. Wink, *Unmasking the Powers,* p. 23.

16. Stanley Milgram, *Obedience to Authority: An Experimental View* (New York: Harper & Row, 1969).

17. Ibid., p. 6.

18. David G. Myers, *The Inflated Self: Human Illusions and the Biblical Call to Hope* (New York: Seabury, 1980), p. 15.

19. Milgram, *Obedience to Authority,* p. 11.

20. Ronald Jones, "The Third Wave," *Experiencing Social Psychology,* ed. A. Pines and C. Maslack, 2nd ed. (New York: Knopf, 1978); P. G. Zimbardo, C. Haney, and W. C. Banks, "A Pirandellian Prison," *New York Times Magazine* (April 8, 1973), pp. 38–60.

21. Peck, *People of the Lie,* p. 216.

22. Ibid.

23. Ibid., p. 221.

24. Ibid., p. 238.

25. Ibid., p. 237.

26. Ibid., pp. 77, 80.

27. Ibid., pp. 241, 246.

28. Ibid., p. 249.

29. Ibid., pp. 241–242

30. Ibid., p. 240.

31. Ibid., p. 250.

32. The political implications of narcissism and laziness are clearly evident in one of the definitions of evil that Peck borrows from his earlier work *The Road Less Traveled:* "I define evil, then, as the exercise of political power — that is, the imposition of one's will upon others by overt or covert coercion — in order to avoid extending one's self for the purpose of nurturing spiritual growth" (ibid., pp. 74, 241; idem, *The Road Less Traveled: A New Psychology of*

Love, Traditional Values and Spiritual Growth [New York: Simon and Schuster, 1978], p. 279).

33. Peck, *People of the Lie,* p. 183. The context makes it clear that Peck means his assertion quite literally. He refers to Satan as "it" in order to avoid dignifying Satan with a personal pronoun.

34. Lifton uses the 1946 United Nations' definition of genocide as "a denial of the right of existence of entire human groups." Lifton claims that the Holocaust, by which he means "Nazi genocide perpetrated against the Jews," was unique in its dimensions, bureaucratic organization, and degree of focus on a dispersed victim-group, but he acknowledges that the Armenian Massacre of 1915 is a significant parallel, including the involvement of physicians; he also recognizes recent examples of genocide in Cambodia, Bangladesh, Nigeria, Paraguay, and the Soviet Union (*Nazi Doctors,* pp. 466–47).

35. Ibid., pp. 6–12. Lifton's basic method in this study was to interview three groups of people: (1) twenty-eight Nazi physicians and one pharmacist, five of whom had been SS doctors in Auschwitz or other camps; (2) other Nazi professionals; and (3) eighty former Auschwitz prisoners who had worked on the medical blocks, more than half of them physicians and most of them Jewish. The interviews were supplemented by extensive reading and consultation in the relevant areas.

36. Ibid., pp. 18, 166, 171.

37. Ibid., pp. 4–5; emphasis Lifton's.

38. Ibid., p. 12.

39. Ibid., p. 13.

40. Ibid., p. 12.

41. Ibid., p. 31.

42. Ibid., p. 481.

43. Ibid., p. 473.

44. Ibid., p. 477.

45. Ibid., p. 34. Asked how he reconciled his work in Auschwitz with the Hippocratic oath, a Nazi doctor replied, "Of course I am a doctor and I want to preserve life. And out of respect for human life, I would remove a gangrenous appendix from a diseased body. The Jew is the gangrenous appendix in the body of mankind" (ibid., p. 16).

46. Ibid., p. 459.

47. Ibid., p. 474.

48. Ibid., pp. 21, 426. Part I of *Nazi Doctors* (pp. 121–144) describes the first four projects; Part II (pp. 147–414) describes the final project.

49. Ibid., pp. 25, 27.

50. Lifton places the word "euthanasia" in quotation marks to indicate the ideologically biased and actually deceitful meaning this term had in Nazi Germany.

51. Ibid., pp. 143, 489.

52. Ibid., p. 480.

53. Ibid., p. 157.

54. Ibid., p. 71.

55. Ibid., pp. 147–151.

56. Ibid., p. 172.

57. Ibid., p. 433.

58. Ibid., p. 73.

59. Ibid., p. 444.

60. Ibid., p. 447.

61. Ibid., p. 196.

62. Ibid., pp. 418, 424.

63. Ibid., pp. 6, 418. Lifton describes the process of doubling in Chapter 19, pp. 418–429, but it is used and elaborated throughout the book.

64. Ibid., p. 210. According to Lifton, doubling is not the same as "dual personality," which is an enduring character disorder that originates in childhood. Doubling is an adaptation to extreme conditions and disappears when the circumstances change, so that after the war, Auschwitz physicians returned to being ordinary doctors, husbands, and fathers. A further difference is that the division in doubling does not run as deep as in dual personality, and the two "selves" are not so alien to each other. Nor should doubling be confused with sociopathic character impairment, which is also more enduring than doubling (ibid., pp. 422–423).

65. Ibid., p. 420.

66. Ibid., pp. 375–376; cf. p. 424.

67. Ibid., p. 211.

68. Ibid., p. 419.

69. Ibid., p. 447.

70. Ibid., p. 432.

71. Ibid., p. 175.

72. Ibid., p. 422.

73. Ibid., p. 442. Lifton first developed the concept in Robert Jay Lifton, *Death in Life: Survivors of Hiroshima* (New York: Basic Books, 1983 [1968]); its functioning in Auschwitz is explained in *Nazi Doctors,* pp. 442-447.

74. Lifton, *Nazi Doctors,* p. 442.

75. Ibid., p. 444.

76. Ibid., p. 443.

77. Ibid., pp. 493–494.

78. Ibid., pp. 445, 495.

79. Ibid., pp. 458–463.

80. Ibid., p. 429.

81. Ibid., p. 498.

82. Ibid., p. 427; cf. p. 503: "Under certain conditions, just about anyone can join a collective call to eliminate every last one of the alleged group of carriers of the 'germ of death.'"

83. Ibid., pp. 502–503. Lifton rejects the common distinction made between person and deeds: "For once a man performs an evil deed he has become part of that deed, and the deed part of him" (ibid.).

84. Ibid., pp. 423–424; cf. p. 418.

85. Ibid., p. 498.

86. Ibid., p. 426.

87. Ibid., p. 500.

88. Ibid., p. 489.

89. Ibid., p. 418.

90. Ibid., p. 4.

91. Janice T. Gibson and Mika Haritos-Fatouros, "The Education of a Torturer," *Psychology Today* 20 (November 1986), pp. 50–58.

92. Ibid., p. 58. Based on their research and previous studies, Gibson and Haritos-Fatouros develop the following model (based on Milgram) for training persons to torture or perform other kinds of social evil: (1) screening to find the best prospects: normal, well-adjusted people with the physical, intellectual, and, in some cases, political attributes necessary for the task; (2) techniques to increase binding among these prospects: initiation rites to isolate people from society and introduce them to a new social order, and elitist attitudes and "ingroup" language to highlight the differences between the group and the rest of society; (3) techniques to reduce the strain of obedience: blaming and dehumanizing victims, harassment that prevents logical thinking, rewards and punishments, social modeling, and systematic desensitization to repugnant acts by gradual exposure to them, so they appear routine and normal despite conflicts with previous moral standards (ibid., p. 57).

93. I am following Walter Wink's interpretation in his series on *The Powers.*

94. Walter Wink, *The Powers*, vol. 1, *Naming the Powers: The Language of Power in the New Testament* (Philadelphia: Fortress, 1984), p. 105.

95. Ibid., p. 5.

96. Ibid., p. 105.

97. Wink, *Unmasking the Powers*, p. 28; emphasis Wink's.

98. Ibid., p. 54; emphasis Wink's.

5. "My God, My God . . . ":
Holy Passion and Compassion

1. *Saint Anselm: Basic Writings*, 2nd ed., trans. S. W. Deane (La Salle, Ill.: Open Court, 1962 [1945]), p. 7.

2. Dorothee Sölle, *Suffering*, trans. Everett R. Kalin (Philadelphia: Fortress, 1975), p. 118.

3. *St. Anselm's Proslogion, with A Reply on Behalf of the Fool by Gaunilo and the Author's Reply to Gaunilo,* trans. and ed. M. J. Charlesworth (Oxford: Clarendon Press, 1965), p. 125.

4. *Process and Reality: An Essay in Cosmology,* Gifford Lectures delivered in the University of Edinburgh during the session 1927–1928 (New York: Macmillan, 1929; Free Press, 1929).

5. Whitehead used the term "sympathy," but what he meant by that we have now come to call "empathy."

6. Whitehead, *Process and Reality,* p. 410.

7. Bernard Lee, S.M., *The Becoming of the Church: A Process Theology of the Structure of Christian Experience* (New York: Paulist, 1974), pp. 155–160.

8. Whitehead, *Process and Reality,* p. 413.

9. Abraham J. Heschel, *The Prophets* (New York: Harper & Row, 1962).

10. Ibid., p. 26.

11. Ibid.; emphasis Heschel's.

12. Ibid., p. 277. The opposite of love, in Heschel's view, is not wrath, but apathy.

13. Ibid., p. 231.

14. Ibid., p. 226.

15. Ibid., p. 277.

16. Cited in Heschel, p. 80.

17. Cited in Heschel, p. 48.

18. Emphasis added, cited in Heschel, p. 113.

19. Jürgen Moltmann, *Experiences of God,* trans. Margaret Kohl (Philadelphia: Fortress, 1980), p. 31.

20. Jürgen Moltmann, "The Crucified God and the Apathetic Man," *The Experiment Hope,* ed. and trans. M. Douglas Meeks (Philadelphia: Fortress, 1975), p. 70.

21. Moltmann, *Experiences of God,* p. 49.

22. Quoted in ibid., p. 46.

23. Ibid., pp. 47–48, and idem, *The Crucified God: The Cross of Christ as the Foundation and Criticism of Christian Theology,* trans. R. A. Wilson and John Bowden (New York: Harper & Row, 1974), p. 146. In support of his translation of Hebrews 2:9, he cites O. Michel, *Der Brief an die Hebräer* (Göttingen, 1949), p. 74 (*Experiences of God,* p. 82, n. 11).

24. Moltmann, *Crucified God,* p. 147.

25. Moltmann, *Experiences of God,* p. 15.

26. Ibid.

27. Ibid.

28. Ibid., pp. 15–16.

29. Moltmann, "The Crucified God and the Apathetic Man," p. 80.

30. Moltmann, *Experiences of God,* p. 16.

31. Moltmann, "The Crucified God and The Apathetic Man," p. 81.
32. Moltmann, *Crucified God*, pp. 273-274. Moltmann correctly cites *Night*, pp. 74-75, but he has obviously condensed the passage, accurately preserving its essence except for the one correction I have made.
33. Ibid., p. 274.
34. Ibid., p. 277.
35. Miguel de Unamuno, *The Tragic Sense of Life in Men and Nations*, trans. Anthony Kerrigan, ed. Anthony Kerrigan and Martin Nozick, *Selected Works of Miguel de Unamuno*, vol. 4, Bollingen Series 85 (Princeton, N.J.: Princeton University Press, 1972), p. 227; quoted in Moltmann, *Experiences of God*, p. 51.
36. Nicholas Berdyaev, *The Meaning of History*, trans. George Reavey (New York: Scribners, 1936), p. 45; quoted in Moltmann, *Experiences of God*, p. 52.
37. Moltmann, *Experiences of God*, p. 52; cf. pp. 29, 34.
38. Ibid., p. 53. Concerning Unamuno's theology of the passion as divine tragedy, Moltmann states, "I can only partially agree, since I am unable to believe that Christ's crucifixion was either a human tragedy or a divine one" (ibid., p. 82, n. 14).
39. Ibid., pp. 12, 31; emphasis Moltmann's.
40. Ibid., p. 12.
41. Ibid., pp. 31-32.
42. Robert N. Bellah, et al., *Habits of the Heart: Individualism and Commitment in American Life* (Berkeley: University of California, 1985), p. 113.
43. Moltmann, "The Crucified God and the Apathetic Man," p. 79.
44. Robert Browning, *Christmas Eve*, V, ll. 23-25, quoted in Moltmann, *Experiences of God*, p. 43.
45. Moltmann, *Crucified God*, pp. 249-250.
46. In this regard Moltmann considers the doctrine of the triune God to be a safeguard against the concept of "one omnipotent God, one omnipotent emperor," such as found in Babylon and Rome. Cf. also Sölle, *Suffering*, esp. chap. 1. Although Sölle shares most of Moltmann's values and much of his theology, she criticizes his concept of the "crucified God" as sadistic (pp. 26-27).
47. Quoted in John C. Merkle, "Abraham Joshua Heschel: The Pathos of God," *Christianity and Crisis* 45 (December 9, 1985), p. 495.
48. Barmen Declaration, art. 4.
49. Moltmann, *Crucified God*, p. 249.
50. Ibid., p. 252; cf. idem, "The Crucified God and the Apathetic Man," p. 81.

6. We Shall Overcome:
Human Communion in Affliction and Joy

1. Henri J. M. Nouwen, *Out of Solitude: Three Meditations on the Christian Life* (Notre Dame, Ind.: Ave Maria, 1974), p. 34.
2. Dorothee Sölle, *Suffering*, trans. Everett R. Kalin (Philadelphia: Fortress, 1975), pp. 68-74.
3. Cited in Daniel Goleman, "Emotional Impact of Disaster: Sense of Benign World Is Lost," *Science Times, New York Times*, November 26, 1985, p. 17.
4. Mardi Horowitz, *Stress Response Syndromes*, 2nd ed. (Northvale, N.J.: Jason Aronson, 1986), pp. 7-42.
5. Sölle, *Suffering*, p. 73.
6. Elie Wiesel, *Night*, trans. Stella Rodway (New York: Hill & Wang, 1960; Discus Books, published by Avon, 1969), p. 63.
7. Horowitz, *Stress Response Syndromes*, p. 41.
8. Quoted in Goleman, "Emotional Impact of Disaster," p. 17.

9. Joni Eareckson with Joe Musser, *Joni* (Grand Rapids, Mich.: Zondervan, 1976).

10. Harold S. Kushner, *When Bad Things Happen to Good People* (New York: Schocken, 1981), p. 133.

11. Richard F. Vieth, "All Things Work Together for Good" (unpublished case study, 1980).

12. Joseph and Julia Quinlan with Phyllis Battelle, *Karen Ann: The Quinlans Tell Their Story* (Garden City, N.Y.: Doubleday, 1977).

13. Sölle, *Suffering*, p. 74.

14. Walter Wink, *Violence and Nonviolence in South Africa: Jesus' Third Way* (Philadelphia: New Society Publishers, published in cooperation with the Fellowship of Reconciliation, 1987), pp. 12–15.

15. Ibid., pp. 15–23.

16. Roland Bainton, *Christian Attitudes Toward War and Peace* (Nashville: Abingdon, 1960). The burden of proof takes the form of a set of criteria that must be satisfied if a war is to be considered just. A contemporary statement of those criteria may be found in National Conference of Catholic Bishops, *The Challenge of Peace: God's Promise and Our Response, A Pastoral Letter on War and Peace,* May 3, 1983 (Washington, D.C.: United States Catholic Conference, 1983), pp. 26–34.

17. Quoted in Leon Howell, "James Baldwin and Reinhold Niebuhr: Responsibility," *Christianity and Crisis* 47 (January 11, 1988), p. 452.

18. Philip Hallie, *Lest Innocent Blood Be Shed: The Story of the Village of Le Chambon and How Goodness Happened There* (New York: Harper & Row, 1979; Harper Colophon Books, 1980), p. 265.

19. Ibid., p. 78.

20. Ibid., pp. 85, 92.

21. Ibid., pp. 89–91.

22. Ibid., p. 96.

23. Ibid., p. 102.

24. Ibid., p. 103.

25. Ibid., pp. 107–112.

26. Ibid., pp. 15–44.

27. Ibid., pp. 205–17.

28. "Facing Evil with Bill Moyers." It is somewhat disturbing to realize that "decent murderer" — the paradox Hallie uses to come to terms with the contradictory sides of himself — is almost identical with the phrase used by Heinrich Himmler to uphold German pride in spite of genocide. Himmler, says Lifton, delivered "orations on the nobility of the German accomplishment in killing so many Jews and remaining 'decent'" (Robert Jay Lifton, *The Nazi Doctors: Medical Killing and the Psychology of Genocide* (New York: Basic Books, 1986), p. 469).

29. Peck, *People of the Lie* (New York: Simon and Schuster, 1983), p. 248.

30. Ibid., p. 266.

31. Ibid., p. 267.

32. Ibid., pp. 247–248.

33. On just war criteria and the difficulty of applying them to nuclear warfare and nuclear deterrence, see *The Challenge of Peace,* pp. 26–62. The criteria of probability of success, proportionality (means proportionate to the just end), and discrimination (no attack on civilians) seem particularly difficult to meet in modern warfare.

34. *Karen Ann,* pp. 193–195.

35. Unpublished tape recording, used by permission.

36. Yvonne Dilling with Ingrid Rogers, *In Search of Refuge* (Scottdale, Pa.: Herald Press, 1984), p. 63.

37. Ibid., p. 242.

Index

Aeschylus, *1*
agnosticism, *53*
AIDS, *62, 122*
Anderson, Bernhard, *31*
anger, *3, 4, 6, 40, 115, 116, 118, 119*
Anselm, St. *86, 91*
"applied biology," *72–74*
Aristotle, *90*
Armenian Massacre, *145*
atheism, *19, 23, 24, 25, 53–54*
Augustine, St., *34, 36, 47*
Auschwitz, *13, 32, 40, 41, 42, 62, 71–73, 75–79, 145*
"Auschwitz self," *76, 77, 78*
Barmen Declaration, *107*
Batzer, Jeff, *15–16, 121*
Beaudoin family, *2–4, 8, 18*
Beethoven, Ludwig van, *12*
Bellah, Robert, *105*
benevolence, divine, *18–24, 39, 41, 45, 48, 53, 86–89*
  responses rejecting or redefining, *22, 23, 39–50*
Berdyaev, Nicholas, *103*
blame, *3, 119*
blaming the victim, *42, 58, 66, 74, 78, 82*
Bonhoeffer, Dietrich, *99*
Browning, Robert, *106*
Buber, Martin, *132*
Buchenwald, *12*
Büchner, Georg, *53*
Buddhism, *42, 50*
Cambodia, *9*
  "killing fields" of, *1, 62, 145*
Cassell, M.D., Eric J., *5–6, 8, 9, 12, 14, 114, 122*
chaos, *27–28, 32, 141*
Christian Science, *51*
Condorcet, Marquis de, *61*
covenant, *31, 34, 88, 89*
creatio ex nihilo, 27

creation, *27, 34, 48, 49, 54*
  myths of, *27–28, 141*
Darwin, Charles, *73*
deception, *70, 75, 78*
demonic power, *28, 30, 37, 58, 72, 82–85*
denial, *4, 116, 118*
depression, *6, 7*
despotism, *25, 39–42*
devil, *29, 85*
Dilling, Yvonne, *9, 135–136*
distancing, *67, 78, 82*
divorce, *7, 14, 115, 122*
Docetism, *91*
Dolores, *13, 45*
dominion, *26*
Donne, John, *111*
Donnelly, Rev. Joseph, *2, 4, 8, 17–20, 21, 23, 54*
doubling, *66, 73, 76–82, 145, 146*
dualism, *25, 26–28, 30, 36*
dukka, 50
Eareckson, Joni, *119*
Eddy, Mary Baker, *51*
Eichmann, Adolf, *79*
Einstein, Albert, *32*
elitism, *81, 82*
Ella, *114, 119, 121*
empowerment, *85, 88, 89, 107*
enemy creation, *66, 69, 82, 125, 128*
Enlightenment, *61*
error, *25, 35, 48, 142*
eschatology, *49, 104, 108*
"euthanasia," *74, 75, 145*
evil, *11*
  apparent and actual, *12, 19, 22, 23, 50, 140*
  definition of, *17, 18, 59–60, 140, 144*
  excessive, *49*

evil (*cont.*)
  incremental, *66, 70, 72,
    74–75, 81, 82*
  institutionalization of, *67,
    72, 74–76, 82*
  meaning of, *18*
  pointless, *49*
  power of, *25, 26, 58, 60, 61,
    63–64, 80*
  premise of, *19, 22, 39, 41, 53*
  problem of, *12, 17–24, 45,
    55, 57*
    see also theodicy
  reality of, *17, 54, 59*
  responses denying or
    redefining, *22, 23, 50*
  social, *64*
  structures of, *25, 36*
  typology of responses to,
    23–24, 25, 38, 53, 54
Fackre, Gabriel, *107, 139, 140*
Fall, the, *47, 48, 57, 58, 83, 84*
fallenness, *25, 35–36*
fear, *4, 100, 115*
Final Solution, *78*
Frank, Anne, *61*
free choice, *20, 22, 25, 26, 32,
    33–38, 47, 56–57, 65, 69,
    71, 79–80, 82, 85, 95, 142*
free-will defense, *33, 34, 36,
    141*
Freud, Sigmund, *57*
Fromm, Erich, *57*
Führer principle, *107, 127*
Fulbright, Sen. J. W. *70*
Gandhi, Mohandas, *126*
genocide, *9, 55, 62, 72–80, 145,
    146, 149*
Gibson, Janice T., *81, 146*
God
  abandonment by, *100–103,
    108*
  anger of, *98*
  apathy of, *90–91, 95, 96, 99,
    101, 106*
  biblical view of, *87–89, 91,
    96, 107, 106*
  compassion of, *90–91, 97,
    98, 99, 107, 135*

God (*cont.*)
  definition of, *86, 90*
  empathy of, *95, 96*
  holiness of, *18, 99, 106*
  image of, *33, 36, 57, 58, 80,
    125*
  immutability of, *90, 101, 107*
  impassibility of, *90–91, 96,
    103*
  justice of, *18, 29, 32, 39, 44,
    45, 88, 89, 97, 123*
  love of, *88–89, 96, 97,
    101–102, 106, 107, 134*
  omniscience of, *94, 95*
  pathos of, *97, 98, 101, 106,
    123*
  perfection of, *92, 96, 106,
    107*
  power of, *32, 88, 89, 96, 106,
    107, 125*
  Reign of, *89, 96, 100, 104,
    107, 108*
  shekinah of, *102*
  suffering of, *45, 90, 96, 100,
    101–103, 106, 125*
  sympathy of, *95, 97*
  as Trinity, *90, 101, 102, 148*
  wrath of, *97–100*
Goebbels, Paul Joseph, *73*
good, *18, 26*
Götterdämmerung, 83
greater good argument, *12, 22,
    23, 34, 39, 45–50, 54, 140*
grief, *3, 4, 6, 7, 115, 134*
Griffin, David Ray, *140*
group, *82*
  group pride, *69*
guilt, *4, 77, 122*
Hall, Douglas John, *34, 142*
Hallie, Philip, *18, 59, 60, 63,
    126, 130, 149*
hardness, *73, 77*
Haritos-Fatouros, Mika, *81–82,
    146*
Hebrew Bible, *28*
Hegel, G.W.F., *41*
Herr, Hugh, *15, 121*
Heschel, Abraham Joshua, *92,
    96–99, 99, 107*

Hess, Rudolf, *73*
Hick, John, *47–49, 57, 140, 143, 144*
Himmler, Heinrich, *73, 75, 149*
Hinduism, *42, 50*
Hippocratic oath, *72, 145*
Hitler, Adolf, *72, 73, 74, 126, 130, 131, 132*
Holocaust, *1, 33, 41, 59, 62, 72–73, 97, 99, 144–145*
Holy Spirit, *102, 108*
homelessness, *8, 123*
hope, *47, 108, 132, 137*
  theology of, *103, 104, 107*
Horowitz, Dr. Mardi, *115, 116, 117*
ideology, *9, 37, 66, 72–74, 77, 80, 81, 82, 85, 127*
idolatry, *83–84*
illusion, *19, 25, 50–51, 56*
impotence, *76, 83*
indeterminacy, principle of, *32*
initiation, *77, 81*
injury, *6, 7, 9, 11*
"Irenaean theodicy," *47*
isolation, *113, 116, 117, 118*
Jainism, *42*
James, William, *50*
Janoff-Bulman, Ronnie, *118*
Jesus Christ, *56, 89*
  body of, *111, 134*
  compassion of 110
  crucifixion of, *45, 89, 96, 100–103, 106, 108, 137*
  cry of dereliction of, *100, 101, 102, 108*
  incarnation of, *101*
  ministry of, *100*
  redemption of, *89*
  as refugee, *137*
  resurrection of, *41, 89, 103, 104, 108, 136–137*
  revelation of, *106*
  suffering of, *14, 90–91, 100–102, 107*
  teaching of, *17, 43, 107, 111, 123–124*
  victory of, *100, 137*

Job, *17, 29, 39, 40, 43, 46, 87–88, 114*
Jones, Ronald, *67*
Jonestown, *83*
Jordan, Barbara, *63*
judgment, *25, 42–45, 49, 142*
  biblical concept of, *43–45*
  redemptive, *44–45*
  retributive, *44–45, 56, 114*
just war, *124, 131, 132, 149*
karma, 42
Kaufman, Walter, *13*
Keats, John, *12, 47*
Keck, Leander, *18*
Kennedy, John F., *132*
Kennedy, Robert F., *96*
King, Jr., Martin Luther, *126*
Kushner, Rabbi Harold S., *1, 15, 28, 31, 53, 114, 119, 141*
laziness, *70–71, 144*
Le Chambon, *126–131*
Lee, Bernard, *96*
Lewis, C. S., *26, 33, 141*
Lewis, Edwin, *28*
liberation theology, *36, 107*
Lifton, Robert Jay, *55, 64, 65, 66, 67, 71–82, 84, 145, 146, 149*
Lincoln, Abraham, *44–45*
Lisbon earthquake, *62*
liturgy, *14, 110, 132–137*
loneliness, *6, 103, 113*
loss, *6–9, 11, 115*
Luther, Martin, *14, 100, 111*
Mackie, J. L., *141*
MacLeish, Archibald, *19*
Manichaeans, *36*
Marshall, Catherine, *52, 53*
maya, 50
meaning, *74, 77, 78, 108, 118, 120, 132, 133, 135*
  loss of, *8–9, 115*
  quest for, *13–16, 19*
Mendel, Gregor J., *73*
Mengele, Dr. Josef, *71, 72*
Milgram, Stanley, *64–67, 82*
miracles, *31–32, 119, 134*

Moltmann, Jürgen, *92, 98,*
    99–104, 108, 148
mortality, *4, 16, 56, 112*
My Lai, *64, 68–71*
Myers, David G., *66*
mystery, *20, 24, 25, 53–55, 72,*
    108, 133
narcissism, *70–71, 132, 144*
natural order, *25, 31–33, 34,*
    47, 56
Nazism, *55, 64, 65, 66, 67,*
    71–84, 96, 126–131
Newton, Isaac, *93*
Niebuhr, H. R., *45*
Niebuhr, Reinhold, *125*
nonviolence, *110, 123–132*
Nouwen, Henri, *112*
numbing, *69, 76, 78, 80, 81, 82,*
    116, 117, 146
obedience, *82*
obedience experiments, *64–67*
omnicide, *57, 63, 144*
omnicompetence, *26, 140*
omnipotence, *17–38, 39, 41,*
    53, 74, 76, 83, 86–87, 107,
    140, 148
  as all-sufficiency, *107, 140*
  definition of, *18, 26, 41*
  as limitless power, *48*
  and logical impossibility, *24,*
    34, 47, 56, 141
  responses rejecting or
    redefining, *23–24, 38*
  self-limited, *31, 34, 141*
oppression, *6, 9–11, 13, 36, 37,*
    57, 84, 88, 104, 107, 110,
    122, 124, 130
original sin, *25, 35*
Ouellette, Richard, *2*
pain, *4, 6, 9, 11, 42, 139*
pantokrator, 17
partial perspective, *25, 51–54,*
    55
Pascack Bible Church, *20–23,*
    50
Paton, Alan, *54*
Peck, M. Scott, *60, 64, 65, 67,*
    68–71, 72, 79, 80, 82, 83,
    131–132, 140, 144, 145

Pelagians, *36*
perfection, *86*
perichoresis, 90
personal growth, *12, 16, 25,*
    46–49, 57
Peterson, Michael, *142*
Plantinga, Alvin, *24, 141*
Plath, Sylvia, *12*
Pope, Alexander, *52*
powerlessness, *76, 89, 115, 117,*
    118, 125
presence, *110–114, 132*
pride, *82*
principalities and powers, *29,*
    37, 83–84
process thought, *28, 35, 92–96,*
    107, 141
Prospect, Conn., *2, 13, 17, 18,*
    20, 21
quantum physics, *94*
Quinlan family, *20, 40, 120,*
    133
Quinlan, Karen Ann, *120, 121*
randomness, *28, 32–33, 35*
refugees, *9, 14, 128, 129, 135,*
    137
regression, *69, 70, 82*
relativity, theory of, *92*
resistance, *37, 104, 110,*
    123–132
retribution, *25, 42, 44*
Ricoeur, Paul, *140, 141*
Roth, John K., *41–42*
Russell, Bertrand, *92*
Satan, *25, 26–30, 33, 46, 61,*
    63, 71, 84, 141, 145
scapegoating, *66, 69*
Schilling, S. Paul, *18, 140*
Schrage, Wolfgang, *44, 46*
Shakespeare, William, *50, 54*
shame, *122*
Shankara, *50*
Sheila, *40, 41, 111, 112*
Simundson, Daniel, *58*
sin, *25, 33–36, 48, 89*
Snow, C. P., *92*
Socrates, *101*
Sölle, Dorothee, *14, 88, 114,*
    116, 121, 122, 148

Somme, Battle of the, *62, 126*
soul-making, *11–13,* 46, 47, 49
specialization, *67,* 69, 70, 76,
    81, 82
sterilization, *74, 75*
suffering, *5, 11*
    definition of, *5, 11*
    excessive, *13*
    phases of, *110, 114–120*
    phase one of (impact),
        115–117, 121
    phase two of ("working
        through"), *117–120*
    phase three of (changing),
        120–122
    pointless, *12, 17*
    positive value of, *11*
    types of, *6–11*
    unjust, *13*
testing, *13, 25, 45–46, 49, 56,*
    142
theism, classical, *89–92, 95, 96,*
    98, 99
theodicy, *32, 35, 41, 47, 49, 57,*
    62, 139, 140, 141
    see also evil, problem of
theodicy of protest, *41*
theology, *84, 108*
    see also hope, theology of;
        liberation theology;
        process thought

Third Wave, *67*
Third World, *9*
torture, *1, 9, 62, 81, 146*
transcendence, *8, 14, 74, 122,*
    132
Tremmel, William C., *61, 141*
Trocmé, André, *126–130*
twentieth century, *1, 37, 61, 62,*
    64, 85, 86, 92, 107, 132
Unamuno, Miguel de, *103*
unjust, *13*
Van Gogh, Vincent, *12*
Vietnam, *62, 66, 68–71, 78,*
    122, 131
Weil, Simone, *57*
Whitehead, Alfred North,
    92–96, 98, 99, 104
Wiesel, Elie, *19, 33, 40, 41,*
    102, 116, 117
Wilson, Donald, *112–113*
Wink, Walter, *36, 37, 61, 63,*
    84, 123, 124, 141
Wolf, Rabbi Arnold, *33*
Wordsworth, William, *92, 94*
World War I, *1, 62, 73, 144*
World War II, *45, 62, 71, 99,*
    126, 130
Zimbardo, Philip G., *67, 81, 82*
Zoroastrianism, *27, 30*